PUFFIN BOOKS
ON TOP OF THE WORLD

Arjun Vajpai became, at the age of sixteeen, the youngest Indian to scale Mount Everest. Always an excellent athlete and a champion sportsperson, Arjun has represented his school, Ryan International in Noida, in various events such as roller skating, taekwondo, basketball, football and volleyball and won laurels for his impressive performances. He is now in Class XII and dreams of even bigger adventures—of conquering the two ends of the earth, the North and the South Poles, of climbing the other thirteen peaks that stand above 8,000 metre and then of ascending all the highest peaks located on all continents. He also dreams of becoming an army man like his father. When not climbing or participating in competitive sports, he likes reading stories about adventurers and explorers.

Anu Kumar's most recent novel is *The Dollmakers' Island* (Gyaana Books, 2010). Her latest book for children, *Atisa and his Time Machine: Adventures with Hiuen Tsang* has also been published by Puffin India. Most of her exploring has been of the armchair variety.

ON TOP OF THE WORLD
MY EVEREST ADVENTURE

ARJUN VAJPAI

with

ANU KUMAR

PUFFIN BOOKS

An imprint of Penguin Random House

PUFFIN BOOKS

USA | Canada | UK | Ireland | Australia
New Zealand | India | South Africa | China | Singapore

Puffin Books is part of the Penguin Random House group of companies
whose addresses can be found at global.penguinrandomhouse.com

Published by Penguin Random House India Pvt. Ltd
4th Floor, Capital Tower 1, MG Road,
Gurugram 122 002, Haryana, India

First published in Puffin by Penguin Books India 2010

10 9 8 7 6 5 4 3 2

ISBN 9780143331728

Typeset in Century Schoolbook by InosoftSystems, Noida

Printed at Repro India Limited

www.penguin.co.in

CONTENTS

1. Beginnings   1

2. The Long Trek Ahead   16

3. A Month between Camps   42

4. On Top of the World   70

Notes on Mount Everest   106

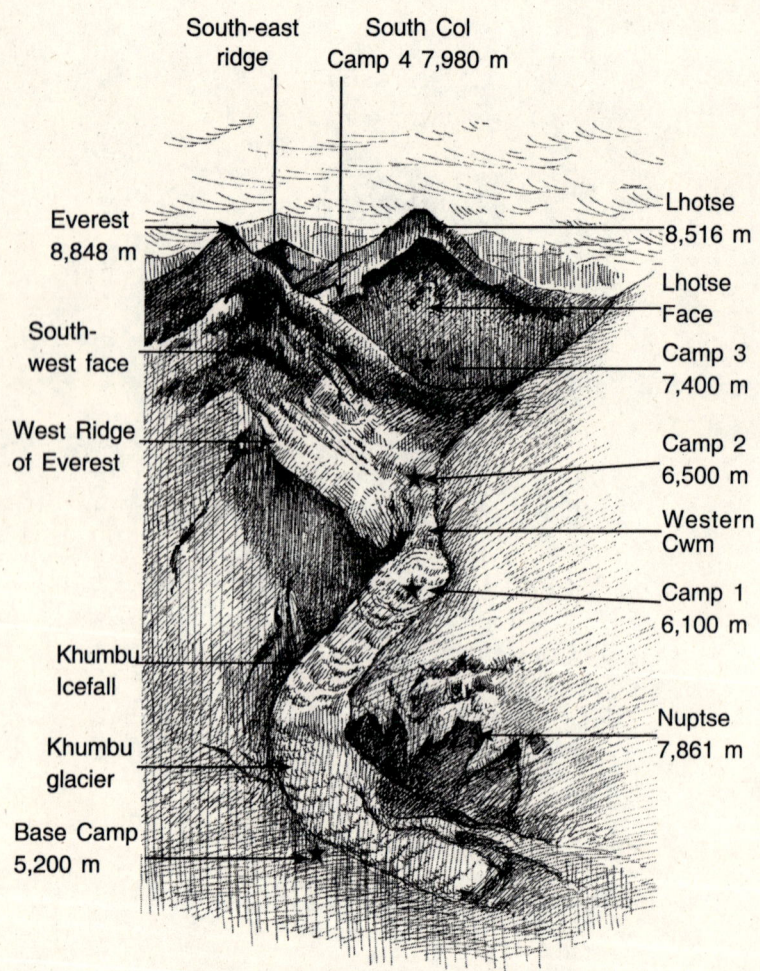

South-east ridge

South Col Camp 4 7,980 m

Lhotse 8,516 m

Everest 8,848 m

Lhotse Face

South-west face

Camp 3 7,400 m

West Ridge of Everest

Camp 2 6,500 m

Western Cwm

Camp 1 6,100 m

Khumbu Icefall

Khumbu glacier

Nuptse 7,861 m

Base Camp 5,200 m

The South Col route to the summit

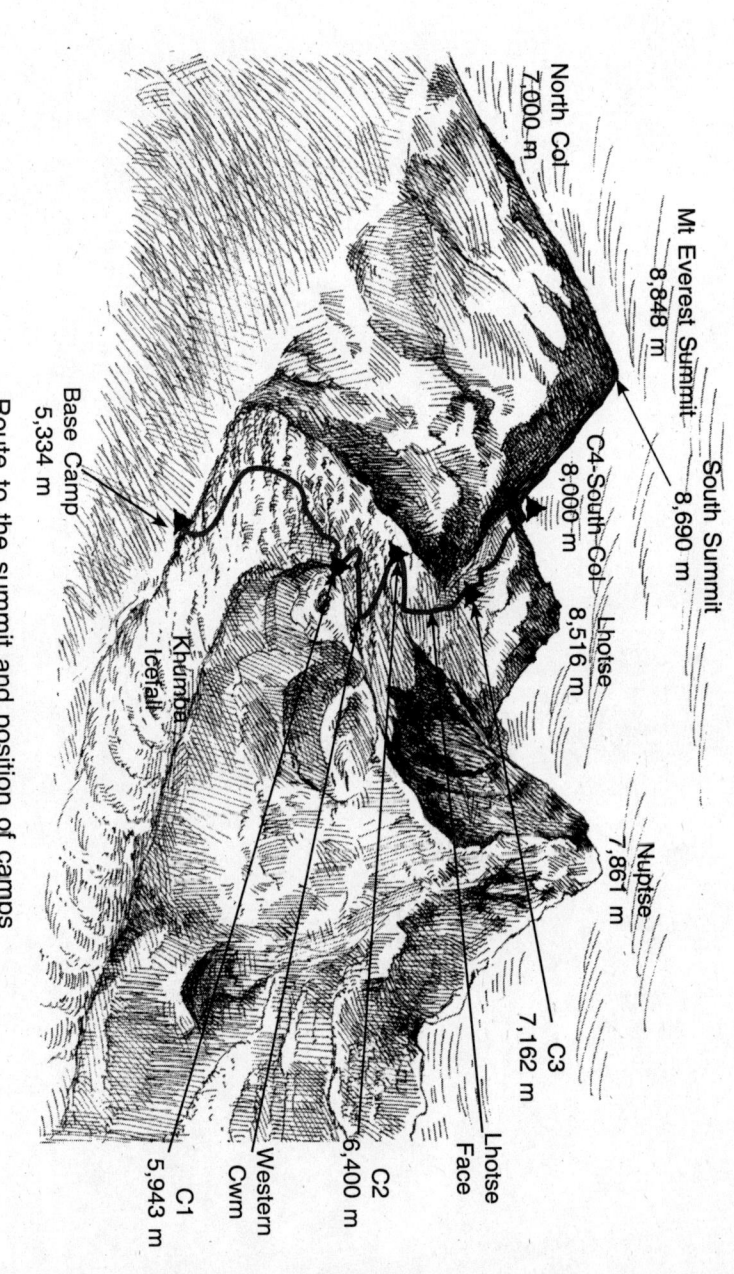

Mt Everest Summit
8,848 m

South Summit
8,690 m

North Col
7,000 m

C4-South Col
8,000 m

Lhotse
8,516 m

Nupse
7,861 m

Base Camp
5,334 m

Khumbu
Icefall

Lhotse
Face

C3
7,162 m

Western
Cwm

C2
6,400 m

C1
5,943 m

Route to the summit and position of camps

1

Beginnings

*W*e had been climbing for eight hours now, our eyes on that lonely snow-clad peak that rose taller than every other around it. We climbed as night slowly gave way and far below, thousands of feet below, the sun rose. In some time, its orange hue would spread slowly over the mountains.

The world's highest peak was now within reach. As morning flooded over the cold snowy mountains, I was finally on top of the world. Nearly two months since I had left home, after three years of preparing, my dream had come true. I stood in the silence, bowing low before the statue of the Buddha placed there by other enterprising climbers.

The Beginning of a Dream

When does one begin to dream? How does a dream develop?

I always loved reading stories about adventure, where people travelled to far-off lands, saw new things and discovered unknown parts of the world. But if you ask me about dreams, I will always begin with this story.

I was around ten when I took part in an expedition to Gangotri, up in the lower Himalayas. This was actually a trekking expedition for the girl cadets of the National Cadet Corps that a family friend, Colonel Jodh Singh Dhillon, was organizing. I had always looked up to Uncle Dhillon; he did so many exciting things; and so when he invited me to come along, I jumped at it. My parents couldn't say no. Partly it was my enthusiasm; but we had known Colonel Dhillon for a long time, and so they didn't raise any objections about my being young and it being unsafe. They just said, 'All right!'

Gangotri lies in the Himalayas, and this was the first time I would get close to the mountains. The snow, the high altitudes, the air that thins as you go higher have a certain magic that take hold of you—ask any mountaineer.

The Gangotri glacier is located in Uttarkashi, almost on the border with China. This glacier is the source of the river Ganga and is one of the largest in the Himalayas. It is about 30 km long and 2 to 4 km wide. All around the glacier are the peaks of the Gangotri Group, including several notable for their tricky climbing routes, such as Shivling, Thalay Sagar, Meru and Bhagirathi III.

I made it with the others to the lower camps, and had lots of fun. Uncle Dhillon regaled me with stories of the mountains that fired my imagination further. He was an experienced army man, and also a keen mountaineer, with a deep love for the mountains. He had climbed several challenging peaks, and had lost his toes from frostbite during a particularly difficult climb.

Since I was accompanying the team as an informal member, I couldn't go beyond the lower camps. But I remember that trip to Gangotri vividly, for it was my first experience of how remote, beautiful and challenging the mountains could be. Since then, the mountains have had a magical effect on me.

To this day, I can listen open-mouthed to Uncle Dhillon's stories about mountaineering, though I must have heard them many times already. In 1987, much before I was born, he had been part of an international expedition that climbed the two peaks (I and IV) of the Saser Kangri, using the more difficult western ridge route. The Saser Kangri, which is part of the Karakoram range, has four peaks, all over 24,000 feet in height; and the two peaks, I and IV, had proved especially challenging for climbers. Uncle Dhillon did it in one-third the time it took the others in his expedition team. His colleague, Brigadier Khullar, wrote a book on it, called *The Mountain of Happiness*.

In 1995, he climbed Mount Kamet, which at 25,643 feet is the second highest peak in the Garhwal region. He ascended it via the more difficult west face, and later spent hours organizing and supervising a rescue effort for one of his younger team members who had fallen into a crevasse. While the rescue attempt was successful, Uncle Dhillon's toes were severely affected by frostbite and he was forced to have them amputated.

Uncle's love for mountaineering remained undiminished despite this. He conceived and conceptualized the first expedition to the Everest by women officers of the Indian Army. He headed the Himalayan Mountaineering Institute in Darjeeling and at present heads the Indian Institute of Skiing and Mountaineering in Gulmarg. He is my role model and inspiration. It was he who recommended me for the basic course in mountaineering conducted every summer by the Nehru Institute of Mountaineering in Uttarakhand, though I was still young by the standards of the average climber. At the two courses I took at the NIM in 2009, I formally picked up some essential skills related to mountaineering.

Tales of mountaineers still fascinate me. As I got more and more enthusiastic about trekking, besides sports of all kinds, I read all I could about these mountaineers who had braved all odds, taken immense risks and succeeded; and my dreams only grew. There was Reinhold Messner, the first man who had climbed Mount Everest without the use of supplementary oxygen; the first ones who got there, Hillary and Tenzing; the tragic story of George Mallory; and of course Apa Sherpa, the man who has climbed Everest a record twenty times. In fact, when he made his twentieth attempt, I was part of the same expedition. But I am rushing ahead of my story!

THE SAHYADRIS

When I was thirteen or so, during my holidays from school, I discovered the hills around my nani's house in Pune. The Sahyadris lie in the Western Ghats, a mountain range part of the Deccan Plateau and older than even the Himalayas. It is largely made up of basaltic rocks. The Western Ghats extend from the Satpura range in the north, go south past Goa, through Karnataka and into Kerala and Tamil Nadu. The Sahyadri range has peaks near places like Matheran, Lonavala, Khandala, Mahabaleshwar, Panchgani and the Amboli Ghat, and offers great rock climbing experiences.

For anyone who dreams of being a reasonably decent climber, an initial rock climbing course or experience is essential. That is why being part of and watching first-hand the other climbers in the expedition to Gangotri helped. An experience such as this familiarizes you with the gear—the ropes, climbing equipment, belaying, techniques to climb various rock formations and rock materials, abseiling, how to find routes to climb and of course the art of rock climbing itself (the skill of using one's legs rather than arms and so on). There are the added after-effects of learning to cope with aching legs, arms, back and fingertips.

Rock climbing adds a whole new dimension to your life. I think for me rock climbing came easily. As a kid, I had always been an outdoor person and loved sports. Even when I was seven or eight, my parents tell me I was always rushing out of home, and most times teachers would find me in the school playgrounds rather than in class.

There was no sport I didn't find exciting. They all offered their own challenges and excitement. I played not for the sake of winning, but because of what it asked out of me. You learn a lot of things about yourself when you play. I won my first sporting medal at roller skating and have represented my school, Ryan International, in various events such as taekwondo and karate. I have also played volleyball, football and basketball at the district level.

I think this early interest in sports helped. Mountaineering is a demanding sport and mountaineers train in a variety of ways.

Swimming, running, cycling, weightlifting and climbing are all excellent ways to improve your physical condition. The ability to endure extreme cold weather and sudden changes in it, the stamina to sustain oneself during long expeditions, and the strength to participate in arduous, exhausting climbs are all necessary for a mountain climber. Mountaineering also depends a lot on teamwork, an ability to trust and empathize. Tales of Everest climbers I read about told me how spectacular achievements were possible when teams worked in perfect unison and understanding. Once you take part in various sporting events, in team games, you learn a bit of this as well.

After practising rock climbing, I followed it up with a class in aid climbing. Aid climbing is a style of climbing in which standing on or pulling oneself up via devices attached to fixed places is used to make upward progress. This introduced me to techniques in artificial climbing and pegs. These skills are especially suited for difficult walls and tricky mountain sections. After climbing for a few months, when I learnt what climbing was all about, it was time for a class in ice climbing. Here you learn to use ice screws, snow belays, crampons and those ice picks that look so cool. One has to wear hard boots and learn to climb in heavy-weather gear.

After all this, it was a good time to join a guided expedition to a high mountain.

The First Test–DKD II

In 2009, soon after my tenth standard Board exams, I joined the month-long Basic Mountaineering Course at the Nehru Institute of Mountaineering in Uttarkashi in Uttarakhand. Uncle Dhillon mentioned this course to my parents and me, and seeing how very interested I was in climbing and mountaineering, he suggested I should enrol for it. The basic course is held every year from 24 April to 21 May. I was thrilled at the end of it not just because of all that I had learnt but also for the exceedingly good grades I got. It boosted my confidence and made it possible for me to enrol for the Advanced Mountaineering Course which the NIM runs from 13 September to 10 October. You need good grades, at least an A, to go for the advanced course which really tests you even as you pick up more skills in mountaineering and climbing.

One of the things that really helped me at the NIM was the climb to the 5,759 metre (18,892 feet) peak called Draupadi ka Danda (Draupadi's Peak) in Uttarakhand. It was the highest peak I had climbed so far. During this expedition my instructors had a chance, first-hand, to assess me and I am glad I didn't let them down.

The feedback I received from my instructors, including the principal at NIM, Colonel I.S. Thapa, was really encouraging. Normally trainees or novice climbers complain of headache and feel nauseous, or else experience stomach ache once they reach heights above 9,000 feet, but I seemed to be unaffected by any of this. My instructors wrote that I also helped other trainees with their loads and managed the climb up to the summit of DKD-II quite effortlessly, without displaying any exhaustion or signs of oxygen depletion. My skills and attitude, my instructors unanimously agreed, would help me in bigger challenges and they suggested I join an expedition to climb Mount Everest. Actually, I had found the expedition to DKD-II really fun. I suppose my enthusiasm impressed my instructors, for in a sport which demands individual skills, the ability to work well in a team is also prized as an asset.

This is one thing I have learnt from my parents. While they never pushed me into doing anything, they were always encouraging about whatever challenge I wanted to take up. My mother always wanted me to aim high. She told me something really funny once. 'Aim for the sun, when you want the moon. If you aim for the moon, all you will reach are the branches of the highest tree!' My parents taught me that any job is worth doing with dignity, but one should always give one's best effort to that and enjoy doing it too.

The courses at NIM and the expedition to DKD-II helped me learn how to deal with cold and foul weather, to pack light, to melt water and prepare altitude food, how to set up camp, what gear to use and how to use it. More importantly, on a climb such as this, one learns how to respond to altitude—what is normal and when to be alarmed. One also learns how to handle various mountaineering problems, and ways to prevent illness that comes from changes in altitude. Shifts in altitude bring about changes in the body and these are vital things to be aware of for any prospective climber.

Climbing the Everest, however, was a different proposition altogether. My parents were really supportive, and yet apprehensive. The Everest stands at over 29,000 feet, far higher than anything I had ever climbed before.

FINANCING THE EXPEDITION

An incident involving a friend, Jai Bahuguna, has always haunted my father. Jai was my Dad's colleague in the army. He died while on an expedition to the Himalayas. By a tragic coincidence, his brother Harsh too met the same fate. Still, my parents, seeing my enthusiasm and the faith my instructors had in me, decided around the first week of February 2010 that they would send me for the expedition to the Everest. But it was already February and the expedition season to the Himalayas begins every year in March, so the time we had was very short. My parents had to arrange funds as well as it was a very expensive proposition. It was very difficult to get sponsorship either from the government or the corporate world in the little time we had, and so my parents reached out to various groups of friends, well-wishers, donors and NGOs, hoping to collect the necessary funds. In a short period of twenty-one days, I saw them calling dozens and more people, emailing others, establishing contact, all in their struggle to find sponsors. In the end, it was my parents who put together most of the funds on their own.

As Mom recounts, it was disheartening to see the unenthusiastic response. Yet my parents never gave up. I appreciate the passion they showed for my dream; it was more heartbreaking for them to throw cold water on my dreams just because funds were hard to come by. As we tried to get together the money, we also started planning for the expedition. Climbing mountains, we learnt, is nothing compared to what climbers face in order to find financing for their dream. Going on a big climb involves hard work and a lot of finance. You need people willing to invest in you, to have faith in your dream. A large part of the cost is the permit fee: USD 10,000. Add to that the costs for hiring Sherpas, the gear, transportations, oxygen and such. A low-budget expedition will still require a good USD 25,000 of you.

It is helpful to join an expedition. A lot of trekking agencies conduct well-organized expeditions to the Himalayas whose leaders are usually experienced climbers themselves. On 2 March, my father contacted Asian Trekking located at Thamel, Kathmandu. The last date to join the expedition was 25 March, and there wasn't much time, but in a way, things were moving forward.

Joining an Expedition

Asian Trekking, which organizes expeditions to the Himalayas, was founded by Ang Sherpa and Dawa Steven Sherpa. Since 2008, it had organized the Eco Everest Expedition, under the leadership of Dawa Steven, with Apa Sherpa as the climbing leader and Nanga Dorje Sherpa as Sirdar or Chief Sherpa. Its focus is on climbing in an eco-sensitive manner, bringing back old garbage, in addition to the expedition's own, besides the human waste produced on the mountain down to Everest Base Camp for proper disposal. They also use equipment that seeks to promote the use of alternative energy sources such as parabolic solar cookers and 'SteriPENs' for water purification.

Dawa Steven Sherpa made his first ascent of Everest in the spring of 2007. The ascent and his journey to the Everest gave him insights into the threats to his roots and inspired him to take up the issue of global warming as well as Glacial Lake Outburst Floods (GLOF) that often happen in the Khumbu Icefall area. The Khumbu Icefall lies at the very head of the Khumbu glacier, which is one of the most dangerous portions on the way to the Everest summit. It lies only a bit ahead of the Everest Base Camp, and is often subject to alarming avalanches and glacial lake overflows. The Eco Everest Expedition was thus designed to draw global attention to the threat global warming posed to the Himalayas and to the Everest in particular. Dawa Steven wanted to introduce a climbing approach that would be eco-sensitive, environmentally safe and also cost effective. I was proud to be associated with such an expedition.

Working with a local trekking agency also helps because they coordinate with the Nepal Mountaineering Association. They will provide you with the papers and permits and get you the appointments necessary, and also the equipment that will facilitate your trek up to the Everest. The expedition will put up an environment security of around USD 4000, which is mandatory these days. The money is returned when the expedition has brought back the trash and empty oxygen bottles from the mountain. Empty oxygen bottles are not the main pollution concern on the Everest. They have instead become quite valuable and popular Everest 'antiques'.

THE 'RIGHT' AGE

Both Ang Sherpa and Dawa Steven Sherpa were very encouraging but they were cautious about my age. They valued the experience I had gathered, the skills I had picked and the good recommendations I had. Due to the immense risks involved, expedition leaders usually refuse to take chances with a novice. They will only organize Everest expeditions for people who have already scaled an 8,000 metre peak elsewhere.

I was then sixteen years and some months old. Dawa Steven warned my parents he would be cautious and would take one step at a time.

There are many opinions on the right age to undertake such an expedition. Depending on your age, people will insist there are some things you can do, other things you can't. At sixteen one is too young, at sixty too old. I was sixteen, and I felt just right. Nepal does not allow climbers who are less than sixteen years old to climb Everest. As for me, my age was never a constraint.

The ideal age to climb, according to most experts, is thirty or thirty-five. But then it is really never too late or too early to do anything. You can accomplish everything you want as long as you put some work into it. Climbing the Everest needs almost two years of physical preparation before you are ready to take it on, so it's more a matter of how fit a climber is than his age. Min Bahadur Sherchan was seventy-six when in 2008 he became the oldest person to climb Mount Everest. For him, it was the realization of a half-century old dream. At the age of seventy-two he began his fitness preparations in earnest, traversing Nepal north to south and east to west on foot. At a medical check-up doctors told him he would have health problems if he went above 3,000 metre. To prove the doctors wrong he climbed the little-known 5,844 metre (19,173 feet) Nayakhanga peak in central Nepal at the age of seventy-four.

PACKING UP

Even though I was raring to go, I had very little time to do my packing. Packing for the mountains is a challenge of an entirely different kind!

Transportation of climbing gear is expensive and also really bureaucratic, as it is trekked and taken over long distances. I needed to pack everything bearing in mind that it would be carried on yaks. Ketchup bottles will pierce, jam jars will leak, sugar granules will end up in the clothing. Everything had to be stored in tight, plastic containers because the smell of leaked food products can be overwhelming.

With everything ready, and plans in place, it was with mounting excitement and apprehension that I set off for Nepal. It would begin with a flight to Kathmandu. While I was excited, my parents and I were also a bit nervous. I came to know later how well my parents hid their nervousness. Mom, for example, would get terribly anxious if she saw those mountaineering videos, till my sister had to tell her to stop watching them!

It is only a short flight to Kathmandu from Delhi, and for me, for all of us, a new adventure was about to begin.

2

THE LONG TREK AHEAD

My journey towards Everest began on 25 March, when I left Noida for Kathmandu, Nepal's capital, located at a height of 1,350 metre (4,429 feet).

It was a packed day at Kathmandu. Accompanied by Mom and Dad, I first went to the office of Asian Trekking, where we met the people involved in running the expedition, its chairman Ang Tshring Sherpa, and managing director, Dawa Steven Sherpa. For the first time, I also met Tshring Phinjo. He would be my 'personal Sherpa' for the duration of the expedition. Tshring Phinjo was a sturdy thirty-seven year old, and had already climbed Everest seven times. He was very experienced, and as Dawa explained, could understand me well (and I suspect, 'handle' me well!). But in a matter of a few days, we became good friends and I began to call him 'Daju', which means elder brother.

THE SOUTH COL ROUTE

From home and back again, most trips to the top of Everest take about two and a half months. Most climbers will attempt to climb Everest during April and May. In the winter, low temperatures and gale-force winds make climbing difficult; while between June and September, the monsoons create intense storms and in places heavy precipitation.

Our expedition, like those Asian Trekking had led in the last three years, would take the South Col-south-east ridge route to the Everest summit. The two most common routes up Everest are the South Col and the North Col-north ridge. Besides these two main routes, there are other less frequently climbed routes. The South Col is technically easier and the more frequently used route. It was used by Hillary and Tenzing in 1953 and the first recognized of fifteen routes to the top by 1996.

The South Col route goes past the treacherous and unpredictable Khumbu Icefall and Western Cwm (pronounced 'coom'), then up the Lhotse wall, past the South Col (meaning 'saddle') and Hillary Step to reach the summit. The North Ridge Route is the second-most popular route, after the South Col route. It's a more difficult climb technically and requires a longer descent at high altitude than the southern route. This route, though, avoids the dangers of the Khumbu Icefall. Mount Everest is located half in Nepal and half in Tibet. During the 1920s and 1930s, climbers usually took the Tibet route to climb Everest, but in 1949, the political situation around Everest changed and Nepal opened its borders, a year before the Chinese government closed Tibet. Climbers thus shifted their approach to the south and in 1953, Tenzing and Hillary finally made it to the top.

KATHMANDU

At Kathmandu, expedition teams usually spend several days buying supplies and arranging travel visas. There is always some necessary paperwork to be done, permits to be obtained, and vital climbing equipment purchased.

Over the next two days, 26th and 27th March, we had to complete a lot of paperwork. Some of us also had to purchase essential climbing gear and equipment, things like altimeters etc. Kathmandu is a surprisingly small city. There are lanes and still smaller lanes branching off from big ones and going from here to there into still smaller alleys. For me it was awesome. Every time I wandered into one of those small streets I would think of the other famous climbers of the world who had walked these same streets and lanes, and here I was, literally in their footsteps. Whenever I walked out of my hotel I used to get this very special feeling! All I thought about was those climbers who had come before me and made the ascent braving all kinds of

ordeals, who had walked down these same steps
and taken the same route I soon would.

Sherpas

For the success of any expedition or climb up
the Himalayan peaks, Sherpas are invaluable.
Besides making up most of the local population of
the area, they are also expert climbers and many
among them know every inch of the Himalayas
thoroughly, as I found out for myself, the more
I spoke to and interacted with Daju. While
Himalayan climbing is now virtually associated
with the Sherpas, just who are they?

The word Sherpa means 'easterners' or 'east-
people'. They came from Tibet and settled in the
eastern regions of Nepal more than 500 years
ago. Traditionally, they were farmers and traders,
but from the 1920s onwards, Sherpas began to be
hired as porters for mountaineering expeditions
and soon became integral to the success of
Everest ventures, and climbers increasingly
employed them for assistance. Sherpa advance
teams are the ones responsible for fixing the
ropes from the foot of Everest to the very top of
the summit. They make it as safe as possible. It
is the Sherpas who carry up the tents and pitch
them, lumber up with countless oxygen tanks,
and again take most of them down. They tailor
this mountain for the many expedition teams
they accompany and who follow them.

Many in the Sherpa community live in the Khumbu region on the south side of Everest. Since the 1950s, tourism has become the dominant source of employment and income in the area. While the Sherpa people retain their belief in the Buddhist religion and many of their traditional practices, this change in the local economy and way of life has also meant changes in the Sherpa culture. Earlier, climbing the mountain was held as blasphemous, but is now regarded as a source of economic opportunity and pride. Sherpas themselves hold many impressive Everest records, including most times it has been summitted by men and women, the quickest ascent and the quickest descent, as well as for most time spent on top.

Before I reached the summit and became at that moment the youngest non-Sherpa to do so, it was Temba Tsheri Sherpa who held the world record for being the world's youngest climber on the Everest. There was also Ming Kipa Sherpa, a fifteen-year-old schoolgirl, who had climbed Mount Everest in 2003 using the North Ridge route from Tibet to circumvent the age restriction imposed by the Nepali authorities.

ON MY OWN

My parents left soon after, wishing me luck. I knew they would worry for me, and that their prayers would be with me as I continued on my journey ahead. Almost every day I would email them from wherever I was.

What follows is the reconstruction of every step of my journey towards the summit from the emails I wrote them, and also from memory. Every bit of the road I took to the Everest, the images, the thrills and the dangers will always remain vividly imprinted on my mind.

28 MARCH

From Kathmandu, we flew to Lukla. This is a town close to the southern face, in the Khumbu region of eastern Nepal, and the South Col route towards the Everest begins from here. On organized treks, most of the Sherpas and kitchen staff will also walk from Jiri to Lukla, albeit in about half the time unless clients are also with them. Although Lukla means a 'place with many goats and sheep', one does not really see very many of them roaming around these days. The flight from Kathmandu to Lukla is one of the most spectacular flights I have ever been on, though it's a short one, of only half an hour. The plane flies over beautiful valleys pock-marked green and grey and brown! In places there are snow patches, at others it's just plain ice.

While most of the essential climbing gear is picked up at Kathmandu, there are some shops in Lukla too, where one can get last-minute items. The town also has lodges where one can have basic Western-style meals. If the required items are not found in Lukla, you can meet with better luck up ahead in Namche Bazaar.

That very morning we began trekking from Lukla that is located at 2,860 metre (9,384 feet) to Phakding 2,622 metre (8,603 feet). We reached Phakding at five in the evening and stayed overnight at a lodge there. It was a simple wooden lodge with just the basic comforts. There are many like this all along the trek to the Base Camp.

From Lukla, most trekking groups will take two days to reach Namche Bazaar, at a nice easy pace to help in altitude acclimatization. This is a term I came across often, for it's an essential part of any mountaineering expeditions —how to train yourself for spending time at high altitudes. In terms of distance, the trek from Lukla to Namche Bazar can be done in one long day (actually eight to ten hours) but is not advised due to increased risk of altitude sickness (another word to remember!).

From Lukla, as we trekked to Namche, our northwards move had begun. For the next month, we would take it a step at a time. Coming face to face with the world's highest peak demands a lot from the body, and a high mental conditioning. In all my previous climbing experiences, I had shown no signs of exhaustion or high altitude sickness, something that had made my instructors at NIM have so much confidence in my abilities.

The road to the top of the world, however, would be the ultimate test.

For me, it was an awesome feeling to get back into the mountains and start trekking. I met other trekkers too. The higher we climbed, I could feel the difference in the air. It felt so fresh and good!

For the next month and a half, I would have to rise at daybreak to begin the day's trekking. In higher altitudes, the sun can be blindingly hot. And still higher, avalanches could melt during the day making things risky for climbers; so we try to get most of our climbing done early on in the day.

Just as we leave Lukla, there is a narrow canyon that plunges steeply to a translucent blue-coloured river formed from glacier melt. Tibetan-style houses perch on hillsides. To get to Namche, climbers move past these Sherpa villages. Most of the houses there have been converted to tourist lodges now. It is a steep climb. The hundred or so lodges between Lukla and Base Camp offer hot showers, even in the remotest areas.

29 MARCH

I got up early again (it was becoming a habit!) at 6 a.m., to begin the trek at 8 a.m. It is a six-hour trek to Namche Bazar at 3,340 metre (10,959 feet). Namche Bazaar, also called Nemche

Bazaar, is located in the Sagarmatha Zone of north-eastern Nepal. The route along the Dudh Koshi river is very beautiful. It is one of the tributaries that make up the fiery Koshi river that flows south-east. Enroute, the Bhote Koshi and the Dudh Koshi rivers merge.

We reached Namche Bazar at 1.30 in the afternoon. I got my first call from home at around three that day. My parents were already back home and am sure they were missing me. Later we explored the marketplace for about two hours. The whole place, as befitting its name, is like a small market area in the mountains! The marketplace was terraced and divided into levels. It was scenic but it became a big task every time you had to go down to the market or return to the lodge!

On Saturday mornings a weekly market is held in the village centre. People from around the area come to sell their wares. The market starts around sunrise and breaks up around 11 a.m. There's also a daily Tibetan market where clothing and cheap Chinese consumer goods are sold. Tibetan merchants travel to the market via the high passes through the Himalayas, even though the Chinese currently disallow this passage.

There are yak trails too, going all the way up to Base Camp, leaving behind them hazy dust clouds. Sherpas leading the yaks carrying the expedition equipment make a musical procession.

Almost everyone trekking in the Khumbu region will visit Namche Bazaar, for it is the gateway to the Himalayas. Visitors are likely to stay at least one night, if not two, for altitude acclimatization. The village has many shops where one can find almost anything required for trekking, but prices are higher than in Kathmandu. The higher you go up into the Khumbu, the more expensive everything gets, so by the time you reach Lobuche at 4,930 metre (16,175 feet), the prices in Namche will appear reasonable. Near the top of the village is the headquarters for Sagarmatha National Park as well as Nepalese army barracks. Many trekkers get up before sunrise to go up to the Sagarmatha National Park headquarters for the impressive views of Mount Everest, Lhotse, Thamserku, Ama Dablam and other magnificent peaks (though you can see these only on a clear day) and to visit the museum. The real trek to Base Camp begins from Namche where immediately upon leaving the town, Everest appears on the horizon next to Lhotse, only 15 miles (25 km) away. It is a wonderful feeling, to have the highest mountain on earth appear in this manner.

30 MARCH

We set out to trek towards Thame at 3,820 metre (12,530 feet). Thame is a small village near Mount Everest. It stands on the old salt trading route that once existed between Tibet, Nepal and India. It is also the childhood home of Tenzing Norgay, who with Sir Edmund Hillary was the first to climb Everest.

The lodge we were to stay in was managed by Apa Sherpa's sister. She gave us a very warm, traditional welcome. As soon as I entered the house, I felt goose pimples on my skin! I could only think that this was the house of the person who has made more Everest summits than anyone else. So I was in the presence, even if Apa Sherpa wasn't around yet, of a living legend! This was where he had spent his childhood and his early youth. During our stay here, we experienced our first snowfall in the mountains.

Apa Sherpa's Story

Apa, whose actual name is Lhakpa Tenzing Sherpa, is nicknamed 'Super Sherpa' and that is understandable. He holds the record for reaching the summit of Mount Everest more times than any other person on earth. As part of the Eco Everest Expedition 2010, Apa made his twentieth Mount Everest summit in May 2010.

Apa's father died when Apa was only twelve years old and so he had to shoulder the responsibilities of his family that included his mother, two sisters and three young brothers. He dropped out of school and began earning a living by working as a porter for mountaineering groups. His career as a climber began in 1985, and he first worked as a kitchen boy and porter for various expedition groups, but he was not given the opportunity to reach the summit until 1990.

Later, Apa moved with his wife and young children to the United States with the help of a friend for business opportunities and to provide a better education to their children. They currently live in Utah. In April 2009, Apa founded the Apa Sherpa Foundation which is dedicated to the improvement of education and economic development in Nepal.

Apa first reached the summit of Mount Everest on 10 May 1990. This was his fourth attempt and he accompanied a New Zealand team led by climber Rob Hall along with Peter Hillary, son of Edmund Hillary. He then began his career as Sirdar, or Chief Sherpa, for many expeditions to the summit. He has since reached the summit every year between 1990 and 2010, except for the years 1996 and 2001. All but three such summit ascents have been in May, and in 1992 he reached the summit twice.

31 MARCH

We were to head for Khumjung at a height of 3,790 metre (12,435 feet) that day. It took us four hours and we reached Khumjung at noon time. It was good to walk on the freshly fallen snow, though I slipped sometimes. When we finally reached Khumjung, I was so hungry I had double helpings at lunch, including two club sandwiches! It was a satisfying day for I got a call from home soon after and then again in the evening!

This was where my Daju's (Tshring Phinjo's) home was, and I got to meet his family. It was Dawa Steven's home village as well. Daju's children were very excited seeing someone nearer their age who was already making an attempt for Everest. There was a bakery where I had loads of chocochip doughnuts. It got really cold in the night and snowed. All in all, a wonderful day! There is also a monastery in Khumjung that supposedly houses a Yeti scalp. Unfortunately, I never got to see it. Maybe next time!

1 April

We started early for Tengboche Monastery at 3,837 metre (12,589 feet). We reached in two hours, though it was a steep and quite a tortuous climb. You first have to go up and then down and up and then again down, lots of up and downs, to finally reach up! Mount Everest appeared closer than ever before, more real and not as part of a photograph. And it was more beautiful than I had ever imagined. I was stunned into silence. The mountain seemed to be calling me towards it. I wanted to touch it with my hands but every time I reached out, my hands came up against nothing but thin air!

Another peak with a height of over 8,000 metre can be seen from Tengboche. This is Lhotse. Climbers vie to summit it because it presents so many challenges. At Tengboche there is a big, old monastery. It was a totally new experience attending the evening prayer. In that half darkness, we felt a strange holy silence descend as the monks chanted the holy prayer in unison, 'Om Mane Padme Hum'. It is a prayer associated with the 'bodhisattva' of compassion, called Avalokiteshvara.

At Tengboche, located high on a knife-edged ridge, the morning views are especially fine. Half the trekkers turn back from here and thus the trek onwards is much less populated. One day, the track looked pounded into a two-inch dust layer by tourists, porters and yak trains but when they left, the effect was sharply different the next day.

Tengboche's Buddhist monastery is the largest gompa in the Khumbu region. It was built in 1923. In 1934, it was destroyed by an earthquake but subsequently rebuilt. It was destroyed again by a fire in 1989, and again built with the help of volunteers and contributions from many people, in Nepal and outside. Tengboche Monastery has a panoramic view of the Himalayan mountains, including the peaks of Tawache, Everest, Nuptse, Lhotse, Ama Dablam and Thamserku. Tenzing Norgay was born in the area in the village of Thani and was once sent to Tengboche Monastery to be a monk.

Once Hillary and Tenzing Norgay reached the summit, this monastery, located on the South Col route, acquired more international prominence as it is on the route to the Base Camp. Those hopeful of climbing Everest visit the monastery to light candles and seek blessings for a safe climb and for good weather. John Hunt, who led the 1953 expedition and was one of the first mountaineers to visit the monastery (previous expeditions had approached the mountain from the northern Tibetan side), had this to say of the monastery at Tengboche in *The Ascent of Everest*:

> *Tengboche must be one of the most beautiful places in the world. The height is well over 12,000 feet. The monastery buildings stand upon a knoll at the end of a big spur, which is flung out across the direct axis of the Imja river. Surrounded by satellite dwellings, all quaintly constructed and oddly mediaeval in appearance, it provides a grandstand beyond comparison for the finest mountain scenery that I have ever seen, whether in the Himalaya or elsewhere.*

2 APRIL

Today we were to trek to Dingboche at 4,343 metre (14,249 feet). I was a bit worried because there was no call from home for the signal was weak. I knew my parents would worry if they didn't get through to me.

On our way we stopped to visit a very famous lama to receive his blessings. The place was fragrant with the smell of lovely flowers. With every breath I took in, I could feel the positive energies surrounding us. One very strange thing happened to me. After he completes all the rituals to ensure a safe climb, the lama calls the climbers close to him and touches his head to theirs and then ties a thread around the climber's neck. When my turn came, the moment he touched his head to mine, he said, 'Arjun you don't need my blessings, your name itself has a lot in it! It will assure you victory.' I was stunned and thrilled. No one had even told him my name and how he made the right guess is still a mystery to me!

Chukhung Valley, where Dingboche is located, lies between several mountain peaks, while Chukhung Ri is a ridge on the southern side of Mount Lhotse. It is often used as a practice climb by trekkers. Blizzards can be common here. The snowstorms descend off the lofty tops of Nuptse and Ama Dablam, mountains around this area, blanketing Dingboche in no time, turning the village into a wintry snowy land in summer and the brown yaks white. The snow flurries add to the mud and make the tracks slippery, so climbers have to be very careful.

3 APRIL

We trek to Chukhung at 4,730 metre (15,514 feet). It is from here that our team veered away from the Khumbu valley towards the Lhotse glacier. The route started to look very different. Daju pointed out that the whole route we had trekked that day was once covered with ice. I was astonished to see that what was once glacier had become a rocky desert. It made me very sad. Before my eyes lay evidence of the devastation human beings had wreaked on nature. I felt ashamed and pained as I remembered the garbage I too was responsible for, stuff I had thrown away so carelessly and thoughtlessly in the past. I felt that nature was literally crying for help. It was a day to make a promise, an important one: to be respectful towards nature and to make people aware of nature's vulnerability and our responsibility in protecting it.

Ecological Impact on the Everest

Even as Everest has drawn more and more climbers since the first successful summit climb of 1953, it has also become increasingly fragile. Besides climbers, ordinary tourists also visit the area. The flood of visitors to the Everest brings in much needed resources as well as infrastructure for the Sherpa communities in the area. There are now schools, hospitals, and stores selling Western made goods and also food. But with the visitors there also came more and more deforestation for firewood, as well as a great deal of waste.

Now, thanks to the increasing awareness of the dangers of environmental destruction, global warming and climate change, evidence of which has been detected in the melting ice in certain Himalayan areas, climbers, locals and the Nepalese government are working in a coordinated manner to protect the environment around Everest.

One of the first steps was taken in 1976, when Mount Everest and the surrounding area was designated the Sagarmatha National Park. In 1979, the area became a Natural World Heritage Site, and the flora and fauna in the park are protected and the collection of firewood is prohibited. In 1998, a private expedition team calling itself the Everest Environmental Expedition removed 1.2 tons of waste from Everest. Most of this was collected primarily around Base Camp and Camp II. While plastic bottles and empty oxygen canisters present an ugly sight, batteries, used fuel cylinders, and human waste pose a greater environmental risk. Other environmental expeditions such as Dawa Steven Sherpa's Eco Everest Expedition continue the effort to clean up Everest.

In 2009, when he climbed Everest for the nineteenth time breaking his own world record, Apa Sherpa spent around thirty minutes at the top, unfurling a banner saying 'Stop Climate Change'. Dawa Steven Sherpa, expedition team leader, had then said: 'We are very excited and happy with Apa's achievement. It will highlight the effects of global warming on Everest. Climbing Everest is getting more difficult and dangerous every year because of the melting ice. The rocks that used to be covered by snows are getting exposed.'

The Nepalese government now requires a $4,000 deposit from climbers that it refunds only if they bring down the same amount of gear and supplies that they took up.

4 APRIL

We trekked to the base camp, called Pareshaya Gyab, of Island Peak which is at 5,100 metre (16,728 feet). There were not many people there, only a few groups.

It was almost ten days since I had left home and it felt a long time already.

The expedition plan was now to rest properly and get acclimatized well. This was the first time during the whole expedition that I felt a bit dizzy and had a headache. It was a sign of 'normal acclimatization', Daju said. I felt comforted by Daju's reassuring words. He said that my headache was natural because we had gained more than 2,000 feet in a day and too quickly. He said I would be fine the next day. But the whole night I could not sleep very well, like I had done so far. I could feel the nerves throbbing in my head. It felt as though my head was going to explode any moment!

5–6 April

We moved from base camp to High Camp of Island Peak, to 5,600 metre (18,368 feet) and came back to the base camp that same day. This was just to keep our body in momentum. At these great heights, I saw the mountain grouse, a bird that is common in these areas. They are small birds and the best part is they can eat anything!

Once again I was happy with my responses, at how my body was reacting to the changing altitude, and the distance we had climbed so far. It seemed an encouraging sign at such high altitudes. I seemed to be holding up well, even after I had been exposed to a much higher altitude than at the base camp of Island Peak.

Island Peak, also known as Imja Tse, is a mountain in the Himalayas of eastern Nepal. The peak was named Island Peak in 1951 by Eric Shipton's expedition team since it looks like an island in a sea of ice when seen from Dingboche. Island Peak was first climbed in 1953 by a British team as a training exercise in preparation for Mount Everest. Tenzing Norgay was one of the members of this team. The peak was renamed in 1983 to Imja Tse but Island Peak remains the popular choice. The peak is actually an extension of the ridge coming down off the south end of Lhotse Shar.

The next day, we followed the same routine. Climbers spend a month or so getting used to the mountains, familiarizing themselves with altitude, to make it easier for themselves when the time comes for the final summit push. These are all rehearsals for the climb to the summit.

To climb Island Peak, one has the option of starting from the base camp which is at 5,100 metre and starting the climb between 2 and 3 a.m. Another option is to ascend to High Camp at some 5,600 metre in order to reduce the amount of effort and time needed for summit day. However, there may be worries about water supply and dangers of sleeping at a higher altitude, and so many prefer starting from base camp for the climb up. Base camp to High Camp is a hike, but just above High Camp there are some rocky ledges and steps that need moderate scrambling. The climb to the summit is somewhat difficult because it involves some steep climbing. There is a massive crevasse on the wall leading to the summit, and ladders have been fixed on the initiative of the Himalayan Mountaineering Association to help climbers. On top, while Mount Everest is a mere 10 km away to the north, the view is blocked by the massive wall of Lhotse, towering 2,300 metre above the summit.

7 APRIL

We started early for the summit of Island Peak which is at 6,189 metre (20,299 feet). We started around 5 in the morning. It was a bit cold, but bearable! After around two hours of climbing we reached crampon point, the place where crampons became essential. This is the place where the technical bit of Island Peak starts. We encountered long ice walls and crevasses, which was why we had to be prepared and had fixed spikes on the underside of our huge ice boots.

Before we reached the top, there was one major obstacle to cross. There was a huge ice wall just below the summit. I was already tired. One could only go on by making the mind strong and with sheer will power. Finally at 11.42 a.m., seven hours after we had started, I was standing on the top of Island Peak. It was an awesome experience!

Instead of admiring the things which I saw, my thoughts were on Everest, that the view there would be infinitely more beautiful. I savoured every moment before I began my descent. I wanted to spend some more time there, but the winds were picking up. Returning became more important because a good mountaineer is the one who can come back in time! While returning we faced one more problem. We had finished all our water supplies and were by now very thirsty. But it was essential to keep going, so we reached base camp terribly dehydrated. I felt more exhausted than ever, and found that I had some temperature. I almost finished one full packet of dry glucose at once! It was a very helpless, difficult time and I was glad I had Daju with me. All thoughts of Everest had totally vanished!

8 APRIL

After reaching the summit of Island Peak, the team stayed back at the base camp of Island Peak the next day. Since we had an extra day in hand, there wasn't much need to hurry. It was more important to rest. That morning, I awoke feeling very fresh. The first thing I did was have lots of water, as I was still very thirsty. Daju was really concerned and asked repeatedly if I was okay. When finally I asked him what the matter was, he replied it was because I had slept for more than twelve hours. His worries vanished when he saw me having my food properly.

9 APRIL

We trekked back to Dingboche. Coming back from the glacier and Island Peak was a big relief. But it was very exhausting! I had thought my body had recovered from the dehydration of a day before, but I was wrong. It did seem I needed more rest and this worried me a bit. Everest was still way off and I was already very tired. I needed to be mentally tougher.

At Dingboche we stayed at Mengma's lodge.

Mengma gave us a warm welcome. She is a tall, elegant woman, with a lot of warmth and friendliness about her. She must be in her mid-forties. She managed the lodge on her own, and she ran it very effortlessly and efficiently. One of my most pleasant stays during the expedition was at Mengma's lodge. I was also very fascinated by her because she too had been on an Everest expedition. It was an experience by itself to hear her speak and relate her stories. When she was in the mood, she could make her stories come alive. We never even realized that an entire day or evening had flown by. It was snowing outside, and the evenings were beautiful, with the bukhari keeping us all warm inside the small wooden room. Even the kitchen staff joined us after they were done with their work. I don't even remember how many cups of hot chocolate I must have drunk, I was so totally lost in her stories. I was like a son to her. She was very worried about me as she had seen the real side of 'the mountain without mercy', because it can be so unpredictable.

One of the stories she told me was from the time she had made the summit trip herself, as part of an expedition. At Camp IV, the last proper halt before climbers make for the summit, Mengma had a dream. She dreamt about the group of climbers who had made it to the top only the day before. As they made their descent, which people say is always more difficult, Mengma dreamt that two climbers had lost their footing, slipped and plunged to their deaths deep in a crevasse. She took it as an omen, a message from the mountain. She knew she had to turn back and not climb the mountain further. The next morning, she followed her instincts and returned to Base Camp and back to Dingboche.

10 April

We were to trek to Lobuche at 4,915 metre (16,126 feet), which is only 8 km from the Everest Base Camp. I awoke to the sound of a shovel raking the ice away from the front path. I was still half asleep when I looked out of my tiny little wooden window. It was Mengma making a small path through the snow so it would be easier for us to go in and out of the lodge. She was doing it all on her own. We had breakfast and were ready to make a move for the next destination—the Everest Base Camp! As we were about to leave Mengma came running up, waving her hand. We had heard her shouting behind us, 'wait, wait', and her voice carried far in the silence, the only other sound being the crunch of our boots on the snow. When we looked back, there she was holding out *khatas*, or Sherpa prayer flags or scrolls for all of us. They are supposed to bring good luck and protect you from difficulties.

I will always remember Mengma. To me, she came to symbolize the close relationship Sherpas have with the Himalayas. In several ways, these great mountains seem to speak to them, even in their dreams. And that is perhaps why it is they, the Sherpas, who are taking the lead now in protecting the mountains which have given so much to them.

After trekking for some time, it was obvious that the real climb towards Everest had finally started. To reach Lobuche you have to make a steep climb. Everest was now closer than ever before. It would be more than a month after this that I would make my final push for the Everest summit.

The tombstones of those who have died on Everest form a long line of monuments a little south of Lobuche. While many climbers have made it to the top, it has killed many others in horrible falls and deep crevasses. It's a mountain that must never be underestimated.

The death zone, for example, that lies above 8,000 metre, above Camp IV, has taken many strong and skilled climbers' lives. Taking on the Everest requires intensive training, and as every good mountaineer has warned, you don't do this in a hurry. One could be lucky and the climb might go well even if you didn't do your homework. But you will certainly notice that Everest, that most beautiful of mountains, can live up to its fearful reputation of being a mountain that shows no mercy, should the conditions suddenly turn bad and rough.

3

A Month between Camps

Between 15th April and 17th May, we moved between different camps, in a process called rotation, to acclimatize ourselves, which means adapting the body's responses to the changing altitude. We also did various short treks, especially one to the Kala Patthar peak. Besides moving between camps, we completed several rotations to the Khumbu Icefall, Camp I, Camp II and Camp III.

Why do we need to do rotations?

This is one of the most important experiences a mountaineer gains when climbing high mountains in the Himalayas. Once you reach great heights, and climb higher, lack of oxygen becomes a major challenge. Even at moderate elevations, many people experience headaches and shortness of breath. Most climbers must use oxygen and will have difficulty sleeping. However, at moderate elevations, the body compensates by producing more red blood cells (that carry oxygen to vital organs) and all functions will return to normal. At higher elevations, symptoms such as headaches, problems in sleeping, could get worse and may also include loss of appetite, nausea, vomiting, dizziness, irritability and insomnia.

When oxygen is severely limited, the body compensates by increasing blood flow to the brain. At extremely high elevations, the brain can actually swell and blood vessels begin to leak, resulting in something called High Altitude Cerebral Edema, or HACE. When this happens, the climber could experience disorientation, hallucinations and even loss of consciousness. Similarly, High Altitude Pulmonary Edema, or HAPE, occurs when fluid accumulates in the lungs. This produces shortness of breath and chest tightness as well as coughing and bloody sputum.

It is always wiser to avoid altitude sickness. This is one of the things experienced climbers and the Sherpas are constantly dinning into you. As a climber you should learn to read your body, and the changes that come with altitude. There is no need to hurry while acclimatizing. You shouldn't climb higher than 300–500 metre (900–1,500 feet) per day. This is why Everest climbers typically make several trips up and down the mountain to increasingly high elevation camps to adjust to high altitude conditions and then return to a lower level to sleep. This principle, called 'climb high, sleep low', lies behind the entire rotation exercise. You might be tempted to go farther, but all it will bring you is headache, sleeplessness and possibly mountain illness in the morning. That is why our team spent over a month moving between various camps.

Something peculiar about altitude sickness is that though it is a condition that can affect anyone above 2,500 metre, regardless of how fit or experienced they are, it affects some people and not others. For example, the Sherpas are able to adjust to higher altitudes better. Some people use oxygen more efficiently than others and therefore adapt better in this rarified atmosphere. Other risks to Everest climbers include frostbite and hypothermia from extreme temperatures, extreme sunburn, and broken bones from falls.

REACHING BASE CAMP

On 11 April we reached Base Camp which is at 5,380 metre (17,652 feet).

When climbers take the South Col route to ascend Everest, they make use of five different camps mainly to adjust to the increasing high altitude. At Base Camp average daily temperatures range between −17 degrees C in January to −3 degrees C in the summer.

For Daju and me, it was a long trek on lateral

moraine, before we reached Base Camp. A bit tiring but good! Lateral moraines are actually debris deposited in parallel ridges along the sides of a glacier. The debris is deposited when the frost shatters on valley walls and is then carried by tributary streams flowing into the valley. Lateral moraines are deposited on top of the glacier and so do not experience the erosion of the valley floor and therefore, as the glacier melts, lateral moraines remain preserved as high ridges.

The Base Camp is like a small village—packed this season with so many climbers, many Sherpas, prayer flags running across the entire length of the camp and the almost constant sound of Sherpas singing! I felt part of it all in no time. At Base Camp we had to set up our tent on places specially carved over a small flat area in the ice. Otherwise one's sleep tends to be constantly disturbed by the sound of ice cracking, slipping and sliding away! During the spring climbing season, Base Camp houses about 300 people, including climbers, Sherpas, doctors, scientists and other support staff. It was amazing to go around Base Camp. Still, one had to be very careful while walking, for at any moment you can slip on ice and then your expedition is as good as over.

Our team, those who had reached earlier, including the Sherpas and some climbers, had soon set up a kitchen tent, a dining tent, a communications tent and then each climber had his own personal small tent. There were already several other teams at Base Camp, from other countries. Satellite phones keep ringing most of the time and the world's languages mix as climbers exchange news between the mountain and the world. You wash your clothes in frozen water, where the ice has to be crushed and you have to work very quickly before it freezes all over again. As the clothes dry, they freeze into strange ice formations at night. The same happens to your hair if wet, and even with toothpaste. You learn to finish your meal quickly as it tends to cool much too soon on your plate.

At Base Camp the sound of frequent avalanches coming down Nuptse, Lho La and Pumori can be heard constantly. I threw silent glances at the Khumbu Icefall that lies just beyond Camp I, and listened as it collapsed with a horrendous crash. Base Camp is a place of great hope, diffidence, frustration, conflicts and life-long friendships. Some climbers will leave, their dream fulfilled, others will have to return home with an unfinished task. This is where climbers begin their true trip up the mountain. This is also where support staff often remain to monitor the expeditions and provide medical assistance when necessary.

From Base Camp, climbers typically train and acclimatize by trekking and bringing supplies back and forth through the often treacherous

Khumbu Icefall. They move between camps, setting up tents, leaving stuff higher up that will be required for the final summit push. The first few days I had fun. I felt I was already very well acclimatized because of which it was easy for me to trek around here!

Base Camp, 16 April–19 April

Some other members of the team arrived over the next couple of days. A few of them were already wary of the Icefall and said they weren't ready to negotiate it. Among the new arrivals was our Base Camp manager Dawa Steven Sherpa. We had two climbers from Finland—Mika and Timmo. Then there were Megan Mcgrath from Canada and Cleo Weidlich from the US, and the living legend Apa Sherpa as well. Marshal from USA managed our communication network. Apa is actually a very small-built man with a cute smile and so very humble too! I was taken in totally by his humility after all that he had achieved. I was amazed that a person of such awesome achievements could be so very down-to-earth. My two fellow climbers, Megan and Cleo, had a permit to climb Lhotse, so at the time of the final summit push, we would part ways for a brief while.

The next day I made some new friends, who were from Finland. Mikko Vermas, Tommy and Yonni were so much fun! Mikko was on a permit for Everest, and Tommy and Yonni were going to climb Lhotse. Mikko was a short guy with a big belly. Tommy was also short but he had a massive nose. Yonni was someone we teased a lot. We called him 'chick magnet' because he was tall and good looking. He took it in good sport! All of them were chilled out but extremely strong and fit climbers as well. I loved spending the whole day at their camp. I soon came to call them the Finnish freaks!

I liked how I was responding to the cold and the altitude, but these were still early days. All the Sherpas, who know the weather and the mountain like the back of their hands, were very encouraging and said I was getting stronger by the day. I completed the day's rotation (going a bit up the Icefall and then back) and reached the pre-decided place with the advance party of Sherpas who would go on ahead. Half the other climbers, however, turned back. They got tired because climbing at that altitude was exhausting and it would only get more so as the days wore on. It is also true that while climbing, you should not overreach yourself or exert yourself unduly. If your body tells you it isn't ready, perhaps you really need the rest and be okay for another day.

Today Apa Sherpa also joined us in our climb. He's a wonderful, very approachable person. The manager of Asian Trekking, Dawa Stevens Sherpa, was also very encouraging about my performance so far. In the other teams there were several well-known climbers and it was thrilling to meet Conrad Anker from USA, Simone Moro from Europe and Megan Mcgrath from Canada, who was in our group.

There was a research team studying oxygen levels at the Base Camp and one day Dawa Steven, finding me just hanging around at Base Camp, took me to their camp. They were monitoring different climbers and the Sherpas for how their bodies responded to the thinning oxygen levels in high altitudes.

As one climbs higher in the nountains, oxygen levels drop to one-third of what it is at sea level. Beyond 8,000 metre, in the 'death zone', the body deteriorates, as its ability to process oxygen sharply declines.

The researchers at the camp were surprised for my oxygen levels seemed as good as a Sherpa's. Already other climbers had shown oxygen levels of 70–75 per cent, whereas mine stood at almost normal levels. They teased me a lot about actually being a Sherpa, because the latter are so very attuned to the thin altitude and the low oxygen levels. I joked in turn and said I was a Sherpa but in a previous birth. This made both my team members and me more confident about my ability to take to the altitude and acclimatize well. Even at higher levels, I was sure I would have oxygen levels of 70 per cent.

I had to stop being overconfident though, and this was something I was always reassuring my parents about, whenever we spoke from Base Camp. Whenever we spoke on the satellite phones, they were reassured about my safety (as well as my ability!).

The first couple of days we spent in practising crossing ladders that are used to get over the crevasses that stretch across the Icefall. I was getting more confident about my climbing. I realized the training I had done back home was helping a lot. On earlier occasions whenever I climbed for more than six–seven hours, my calf and leg muscles would ache terribly; but I wasn't affected by anything like this now. Besides, my climbing techniques had also improved; I took to the technical slopes quite easily and confidently. And though these were initial days, I felt I had acclimatized really well, due to which I was feeling healthy and so far had had no headaches.

I was encouraged by this because Base Camp is the beginning of the real test. For instance, if you flew here directly in a helicopter, you would be unconscious in hours, and perhaps dead soon thereafter. But by walking here, our bodies had begun the process of getting acclimatized.

Only a few steps outside Base Camp is the weirdest place I have ever been to. Huge boulders are strewn everywhere. Yet the views are simply beautiful. But it really takes a lot out of one's body. The lungs burst for air, wounds don't heal because the blood flows slowly and is thick, ulcers erupt, nails split and headaches happen with regularity. You lose weight as your muscles waste. And the slightest exertion leaves you breathless.

It's not surprising. At 5,300 metre, we were above the level where human populations live permanently. It's a harsh environment where nothing grows. It's surprisingly warm in the day yet night-time temperatures plunge to −12 degrees C. The Khumbu Icefall isn't too far away and sometimes I found myself woken up by the ice cracking beneath the tent. The rumble of avalanches is never far away. Yet clear nights reveal a sky full of stars and a backdrop of breathtaking beauty with the mountains of Everest, Lhotse, Nuptse and Lhola reaching high above into the night sky.

18 APRIL

The Puja

We had a puja on this day in the Base Camp which is a tradition followed by all climbers and expedition teams. The plan was to then begin the rotation proper and spend a night at Camp I, which is across the Icefall. All mountaineers offer prayers to the deity at the Base Camp. The deity is the personification of Sagarmatha, the mother goddess, as the Sherpas call Mount Everest. It is to propitiate nature at its most remote and barren, and symbolically ask for permission to make the ascent.

All mountaineers offer prayers. It is an acceptance of local customs. It is also an understanding of a fact: that man forever seeks to tame nature, but nature can be difficult to comprehend. These prayers are to that awesome aspect of nature, and an attempt to evoke understanding.

Bells chime, Buddhist prayers are chanted, and rice flakes are scattered. Climbers also throw tsampa, or buckwheat flour, into the air as the lamas conduct the ceremony. After the lamas are done with reading the sacred verses from their scriptures, the Sherpas perform a traditional dance. It's a very slow dance. I think the reason behind a slow dance is that it would be very difficult to do complicated dance steps at that altitude when there is so little oxygen to go around!

Collecting Waste

At Base Camp, among the more exciting things I did, which also made me feel responsible, was the garbage I collected. There are tons of garbage left behind by previous expedition teams.

My expedition was also a clean-up expediton. So all the climbers and Sherpas had to collect garbage. To collect more garbage, there is a system that is followed called simply 'weigh and pay'. Each member is paid according to the garbage they manage to gather, at the princely rate of Rs 100 per kilo! Once, when I was walking around Base Camp, I noticed something stuck deep in the ice. It excited my curiosity. On a closer look, to my surprise, I found it was a helicopter part. I had learnt about a helicopter that had crashed thirty-seven years ago, in 1973, at Camp I. Over a period of time as the glacier shifted, the ice of Camp I had now moved towards Base Camp. I was very excited of course. I ran back to camp and told Daju about it.

So the next day the two of us went to the same place and got to work! After four hours of hard work with our ice axes, we finally managed to extricate the part. And it was no ordinary part; it was the main rotor part of the helicopter. When the time came for the team to weigh and pay us, everyone was amused to see the huge part we had managed to bring in. When it was weighed, the person operating the scales was amazed as he shouted out loud, 'It's 40 kilos!' Daju and I were really happy and both of us divided the money, getting a sum of Rs 2,000 each.

This was one of the many rules I learnt once on Everest territory. With your Sherpa, you work as a team and do not take unnecessary risks on your own. You have to trust your Sherpa totally, as I did Daju; he is your guide, friend and counsellor.

19 APRIL

First Rotation

A day after the puja ceremony, we did our first rotation. This meant going halfway up the Icefall and then back. Our target was to climb some way up the Khumbu Icefall. I was very excited and a bit scared too. It was the first time I was going to step on Everest's main flanks.

The Khumbu Icefall that lies beyond Base Camp can only be traversed with the aid of ropes and ladders. The Icefall is at a height between 5,500 metre to 6,100 metre (18,000 feet to 20,000 feet) and even with all safety precautions, this section is extremely dangerous. Shifting ice under the feet, deep crevasses and avalanches have killed many climbers and Sherpas here. The Icefall contains enormous ice seracs, often larger than houses, that dangle precariously over climbers' heads, threatening to fall any moment without warning.

The Icefall is like a waterfall, moving deceptively. The slope leading down from the Western Cwn, which is the valley between the great peaks, collects vast amounts of snow and ice. The ice flows down and as it reaches the very bottom of the Cwm the layers of ice compact into a deep, slow moving torrent, visible in the Icefall. As the temperature fluctuates, the ice opens and closes enormous crevasses, or fissures, which swallow and grind up anything it catches.

Most climbers simply concentrate on getting out of there as fast as they can. In order to help climbers traverse the crevasses the Sherpa Sirdar and his team, usually from the Nepal Mountaineering Association, fix aluminium ladders across the crevasses. The climbers then cross the precarious span with their fingers crossed and prayers on their lips.

Wherever necessary, we clipped in to ropes as we climbed. At difficult parts fixed with old rope, we clipped in to several lines at once. Almost yearly climbers die in the Himalayas due to old rope. You soon learn to pull at the ropes before clipping in, and not climb with large numbers of climbers on one rope. Later, on steep climbs such as the Lhotse wall, which was a particularly difficult experience, we soon learnt that it was necessary to use our jumars as well as crampons and of course our legs!

All this caution is important, more so in places like the Khumbu Icefall. Many climbers meet bad luck and slip off the ladders, or a fissure suddenly opens wide and swallows them entirely. The drop is steep, often 100–200 feet, and rescue is just impossible. Slowly the ice continues to shift, grinding the unfortunate victim's body, and quickly closes up leaving no trace. Years later, as the ice melts and continues shifting, the frozen and broken remains of the unlucky climbers will stick out from that icy cover, soon to be swallowed up again.

The Icefall should be climbed early in the morning. It's best not to leave Base Camp later than 6 a.m. The Icefall sees some melting later in the day, especially in summer, and avalanches become more frequent. The heat in the morning also makes it uncomfortable. Once through the Khumbu Icefall, climbers reach Camp I at 6,065 metre (19,900 feet).

On 19 April, with other climbers from our expedition team, including Mika, Timo, and Megan, we began our climb around 6 a.m. It was still dark and with our headlamps on, we were ready to go. I began, taking each step very carefully. Timo soon got left behind. Mika and I were together and we set a very good pace. We took some pictures at our first rest point; but as soon as we were about to start again, Mika began to cough badly! Then he suddenly threw up.

He blamed the coffee he had had earlier in the morning. But the coughing fit and his being subsequently a bit unwell meant he had lost a lot of energy, and he decided to return to Base Camp. Daju was, however, very happy with my speed. I was walking at my own normal pace. In no time, as we walked on, we had reached the field in the Icefall which was our destination for the day, criss-crossed with crevasses. It was nerve-wracking to cross these. Some were so deep that we were afraid of looking down. We reached our destination at around 10.30 a.m. We rested there for some time. I ate the apples

On top of the world . . . on the summit. (*Picture taken by Eliya.*)

With Daju's family in Khumjung.

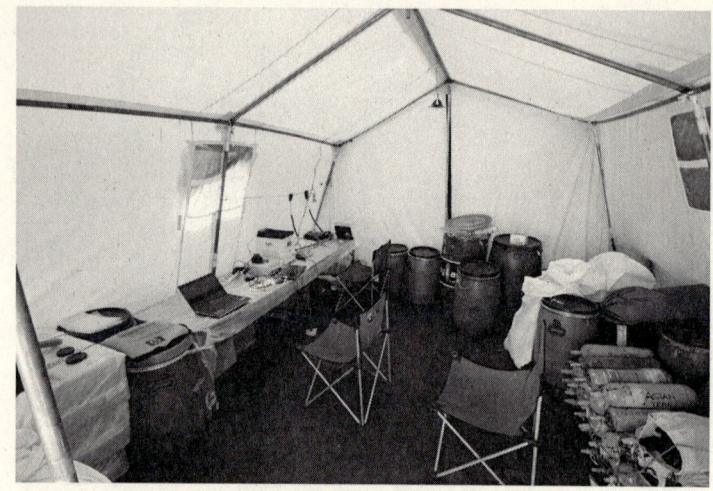

The communications tent set up at Base Camp, our only point of contact when on the mountains.

Puja at Base Camp. All the gears were kept near the stupa so that they are blessed by the mountain goddess.

Crossing a crevasse on a ladder just before reaching Camp I.
(*Picture taken by Mika.*)

The dangerous Khumbu Icefall. Due to the sun's strong reflection,
we sweat it out while crossing the glacier.

Going up the Khumbu Icefall. (*Picture taken by Mika.*)

After crossing the treacherous Khumbu Icefall. (*Picture by Mika.*)

View of the Yellow Band, Geneva Spur, Camp III and Lhotse wall from Camp II.

Daju and I in Camp II.

Climbing the Lhotse wall which is almost at an 80 degree angle. Ahead Camp III is on fire! (very fast winds are blowing up the snow). *Picture by Mika.*

View from Camp IV, the last bit of Everest. Sublimation clouds are forming over Everest (when ice turns into clouds directly without turning into liquid.)

My whole group. Mika, Me, Chinu, Timo, Mamta, Bhagyashree, Apa, Megan, Dawa Steven (left to right; *picture by Marshall).*

An evening view—the setting of the sun and the rising of the moon together is a spectacular sight.

Apa Sherpa and I at Base Camp after the successful summit attempt. (*Picture by Marshall.*)

The unforgettable view from the summit where the Earth bends from all sides, and I could now see that the earth IS round!

which our Base Camp cook had given us and then we began to make our move back. On our way, we saw Timo nearing the field, and we smiled at each other.

The descent was good. Now for the first time I noticed a change in everyone. Some of my teammates and fellow climbers who were worried about me were more relaxed after seeing my performance in the first rotation. Our plan was to rest for a few days and then go for a second rotation which included sleeping one night at Camp I, moving on to Camp II the next day and then returning to Base Camp.

20 APRIL

Second Rotation

It was a clear night on 19 April, slightly windy, but it didn't look like it was going to bother us much. We were to do our second rotation the next day. We would go up till Camp I and spend the night of 20 April there. We reached Camp I in five hours, having set off early in the morning. We could have reached faster but we had a 'traffic jam', with lots of climbers from other expeditions on their way to Camp I as well. Still, it was pretty good considering it was the first time we were on that stretch, Daju said.

Camp I is at an altitude of 6,065 metre. Even at this altitude I did not suffer any headaches. Mika was still suffering from a minor headache, but he said he would be fine by the next morning when we would start towards Camp II. That night at Camp I was not good. Mika didn't feel well, and I wasn't able to sleep either. I had my mp3 player full of popular Bollywood songs. Mika appeared to enjoy them, though he obviously didn't understand a word! But still it helped by making me feel relaxed and by boring Mika enough to make him fall asleep.

The plan to stay in Camp I was mainly because we had to acclimatize. If we hurried, we could lose too much energy too quickly. In Camp I, the food wasn't so good and the facilities poorer as compared to Base Camp. Camp II was supposed to be better, like Base Camp. In Camp I not only are the living conditions bad, but the wind is fierce; we had to melt snow for drinking water here. All my load required for the summit push later had already been brought here, and would be transferred to Camp II and further on by our team of Sherpas.

The area beyond Camp 1 is called the Valley of Silence. At 6,100 metre to 6,400 metre (20,000 feet to 21,000 feet), it is also known as the Western Cwm. This is a flat area of endless snow, deep crevasses and mountain walls frequently visited by avalanches. It is here that for the first time, just a few steps around a corner, that climbers gain their first close sight of the Everest summit.

21 APRIL

We got up early and began getting ready for the trek to Camp II, but somehow my body felt low on energy. Mika too felt somewhat the same. It was a very windy early morning and my stomach did not feel too good. We hadn't slept well, so both of us were a bit tired first thing in the morning. We just managed to cook ourselves some noodles, but we knew this would not suffice for our energy requirements. It was almost like the real climb had finally begun for us.

However, Daju was very persuasive. He said, 'Let's see how far can we go.' The plan was to go to Camp II and then return. I didn't want to, but I fell in with Daju's directions. 'What's the harm in trying?' I said in agreement and so we started walking slowly. In no time, it became very difficult to walk as the winds were as strong as 50 km/h. It was really hard to breathe as well. Mika and I were together, and our Sherpas a bit ahead walking together. After about an hour I began feeling even weaker. My steps faltered and I slowed down considerably. I called out to Daju and as soon as he turned back towards me I threw up! The next moment I was on my knees, totally exhausted.

It had been a hard, exhausting climb so far, and the altitude had made me feel more unwell. Maybe the change in altitude had killed my appetite. The weather conditions were also not good. The noodles I had eaten before starting my climb were now indigestible! After I threw up, I felt even more depleted of energy.

Daju was reassuring. 'No problem, we will go back and try next time,' he said. We started walking back towards Camp I when Mika also joined me. He wasn't feeling good either. We turned back at an altitude of 6,350 metre. Not too far away, with a certain bitter-sweet feeling, we could see Camp II, but that day we were not going to make it there.

The next day, 22 April, we decided to rest at Base Camp.

23 APRIL

I had a good sleep at Base Camp, and woke up feeling much better, my exhaustion of the previous few days completely gone. I even had a hot shower. Mika and I spoke to Naga, who was the Chief Sherpa or the Sirdar as well as to Apa Sherpa. They warned that the weather would only get worse after 26th or 27th April, so our third rotation was scheduled for the next day. I decided to grab as much rest as I could for the day ahead.

24 APRIL

Third Rotation

On this rotation, we were to go to Camp II straightaway and spend a night there. The next day, we would go halfway to Camp III because the route was not open yet. Usually the Icefall doctors go up ahead and check the routes for safety before declaring them 'open'. Camp III is at an altitude of 7,300 metre, but we would only go till 6,770 metre.

After reaching Camp I we rested for some time and started to walk again towards Camp II. The valley was a big snow field. After walking for about an hour, we could see Camp II, though it still seemed a long way off. It was a very long and monotonous walk. The entire Western Cwn was like a furnace. The sunlight that came ricocheting off the mountain walls makes you feel really hot. It was very tiring because after walking for a long time we could see Camp II ahead but it took us ages getting to it; and finally we did!

Camp II is at a height of 6,400 metre (21,000 feet). It is almost at the foot of the icy Lhotse wall and is really stunning. Clouds move in from the lower reaches of the Himalayas and up the valley. While acclimatizing, we spent time looking for cool old climbing gear left here by climbers from Everest's climbing history. This is also the last chance to get a decent, prepared meal. We ate all we were handed because soon we'd be surviving on instants only.

We were careful not to camp close to the Everest face, since there are avalanches once in a while. Although tempted to idly hang around

camp, some of us took walks to the Lhotse
Face to speed up acclimatization and relieve
altitude problems. The walks force one to breathe
deeper and faster, thus filling the body with
more oxygen. Lhotse is a 27,920 feet mountain
bordering the Everest, and its face is a steep,
shiny icy wall. Technically it is a difficult peak
to climb; one misstep could cost you your life.

25 APRIL

We started from Camp II around 10 a.m., and
the weather really held. We just had to walk
for about two hours so we started late. We were
going to climb to an altitude of around 6,770
metre, which is closer than ever to the base of
the Lhotse wall. On the way, we came across
a dead body. It was that of a Kazakh climber.
He looked as if he was just resting, just another
climber sitting by, catching his breath.

It was the first time I was seeing a dead body
on the mountain, and believe me, it can be a
very unsettling experience. Daju told me that
this climber from Kazakhstan had died last
year. He didn't seem to be in good shape as he
lay there, his entire body dislocated. It was a
horrible sight! I had always been drawn to the
adventure and the thrill of climbing, but seeing
the dead climber lying helpless like that made
me aware of the perils of climbing as well.

As we walked on, I felt the shift in altitude, the sudden thinness in the air I was breathing in. It was fun! I had to keep telling myself to go on, and my body was now responding well too. The closer we got to the summit, the challenge became more exciting and demanding. The Sherpas after seeing me climbing began saying that maybe I could do it without oxygen! Of course I didn't believe that was possible, but still it was nice to hear such things.

26 APRIL

The night before, I didn't sleep well for I was troubled by thoughts of that dead climber. I had told myself that such things don't affect you if you don't let them but they do hit you after a while, when your mind is totally free and you think over the day's events. I just couldn't get the climber, as if sitting peacefully, out of my mind.

So far though, it had been a pretty good rotation. Everything had gone well. We soon returned safely to Base Camp, Daju and I being the fastest to make it back. I was feeling fitter and had put on some weight as well, which was unusual because the more time you spend on the mountains, you actually lose weight. We were going to rest for a couple of days before commencing the next rotation.

30 April

Fourth Rotation

We started from Base Camp at 4 a.m. The weather wasn't good. It was snowing lightly but the winds were not so fast. It was a bit easier, unlike the last rotation, to walk on the Icefall area because only a little snow had fallen on the slopes. All of us were carrying the same amount of load so we reached Camp I in five and a half hours. But this was not our final destination for that day. We were aiming for Camp II, another two hours' walk away. The climb this time through the Western Cwm was tough. I was exhausted after the climb to Camp I but we still had to go on. However, soon my body got into a momentum of its own and I started to breath in a particular way. I noticed that if I kept my body high on oxygen from the very beginning, a process which is quite tiring for the lungs, I felt better and more energized. By the time we finally reached Camp II, all of us were very tired. In high altitudes, with so little oxygen, exhaustion catches up very fast.

I was glad I still had my appetite, and was eating much the same way I always did, so I felt good and more confident about myself.

1 May

A rest day. Depending on the weather, we were going to complete our last rotation the next day. This involved sleeping in Camp III for one night. I liked being in Camp II though. It was a good and comfortable place, just like Base Camp. There were many groups besides ours, waiting for the right weather to come up. In Camp II, we had our own separate tents, there was even a mess tent here, but it did not have a heater like Base Camp. The food wasn't strikingly good either, but once you are into mountaineering, you have to say goodbye to your usual creature comforts! One has to rough it out and I was used to it already.

It was very cold outside. In the night, we could not even go out of our tents to relieve ourselves. We had been given 'rest top bags' that help dissolve the excreta. This was the environmentally right thing to do. We also had our urine bottles that invariably froze in the night. Basically it was getting harder to survive up in the mountains and we were in for more testing times. Of course, as the days passed, we were nearing the summit, and it was exciting too.

2 May

The weather suddenly deteriorated. Heavy snow had fallen all through the night. We could not begin climbing that day. Camp III seemed even more tough to get to. First, we had to negotiate the steep Lhotse wall. This stretches to about 300 metre; imagine a wall of ice of that height! Besides, it was full of blue ice that is very hard to get a grip on.

3 MAY

The weather lifted a bit. Apa Sherpa in fact said it was very good weather. So we started getting ready for the final destination of our last rotation—Camp III. We started climbing at 10 a.m. In the beginning, the going was good, though I was just a bit nauseous. Then the wind started to pick up. While it's usual in the mountains to have fast winds, I hadn't anticipated what I would be in for. Climbing very slowly and steadily we managed to reach the Lhotse wall. Camp III was just 300 metre from here. But this last stretch proved to be one of the most difficult to climb. In such harsh weather, the wall was even more difficult to climb. When the climber in front of you is ascending, massive chunks of ice come straight on to you. Also, like I said, blue ice is hard to get a grip on. If you try hard and reach out with your jumar (ascenders), the whole sheet of ice can shatter and fall. So a climber has to be just next to perfect.

At 1:30 p.m. I was just around 50 metre up on the wall, and jet stream winds were blowing very strongly. These winds are common on Everest and for climbers they can be extremely dangerous. The jet stream winds vary in speed from 80 to 120 miles per hour and bring the temperatures shooting down to at least –40 degrees C in no time. I could see Daju's face. He did not seem at all happy about this. We made contact with Camp II, and Apa Sherpa advised us to immediately turn back.

That day, we were unable to reach Camp III because of the weather conditions. We stayed in Camp II for the rest of the day. Though we could not complete this rotation, we learnt later that the weather had worsened, and turning back was perhaps the wisest and most sensible thing to do.

4 MAY

We were all totally exhausted. We could not make another attempt for Camp III as the weather continued to remain inclement. So we decided to return to Base Camp. Our plan now was to rest in Base Camp for over a week. We could not go back up again before the summit push. The weather simply didn't look promising.

5 MAY

We returned safely to Base Camp, where we had a look at the weather report. It was good that we descended that day instead of continuing to climb to Camp III because soon after, thanks to the wind and the heavy snowfall, the whole of Camp III and Camp II had been buried under four feet deep snow. We had indeed been very lucky! For another five days we waited for the weather window to clear. During this period we received the very tragic news that two Russian climbers had lost their lives while attempting to reach the summit during the bad weather.

In the time we spent at Base Camp, some of us also trekked up to Kala Patthar.

Kala Patthar

Leaving Base Camp, a group of us walked up Kala Patthar, a 5,600 metre peak with great views of the summit of Everest. (From the Base Camp you can't actually see Everest.)

Kala Patthar means 'black rock' in Hindi and it appears as a big brown bump below the impressive south face of Pumori (7,161 metre). Pumori means 'Unmarried Daughter' in the Sherpa language, and this was how it was named by George Mallory, the famed British climber who died trying to make the Everest summit in 1924. Climbers sometimes refer to Pumori as

'Everest's Daughter'. Many trekkers in the region of Mount Everest will attempt to summit Kala Patthar, since it provides the most accessible point to view Mount Everest and is just a trek away from Base Camp. The views from almost anywhere on Kala Patthar, of Everest, Lhotse and Nuptse, are spectacular.

4

On Top of the World

George Mallory, who died tragically on an expedition to the Everest, once famously replied to the question 'Why do you want to climb Mount Everest?' with the retort: 'Because it's there,' which has been called the most famous three words in mountaineering.

I had been on the mountains for over a month now. There had been difficult moments, but on the whole I felt happy and accepted. For it is when you have been on the mountains a long time that you really understand them well. And in a way the mountains understand you too.

This is the hidden secret that all mountaineers know. The Sherpas have their own beliefs about the Himalayas and the magic of the Everest. Those frequent climbers know when to go ahead and brave odds and when not to take chances. They have this belief that for all the skills and abilities a climber could have, in the end, you need a strange kind of luck to make it to the top. Old-time Sherpas and experienced climbers believe that it is the mountain that decides who should go up, who should scale summits successfully and who must try their luck another time.

There have been over 4,100 ascents to the summit by about 2,700 individuals. But by the end of 2009, Everest had claimed 216 lives too, including eight who perished during a freak 1996 blizzard that struck unexpectedly on the mountain.

That is why it is important, especially once in the higher reaches of the mountains, to respect the weather. The Everest is beautiful but it can also be extremely inhospitable and unpredictable as these unfortunate climbers found out to their cost. One never knows when bad weather may strike. And what looks like an easy climb on a sunny day can turn into something horrible, so it's important to be prepared at all times.

The mountain creates its own weather, and is impossible to predict accurately. Blizzards can happen suddenly and the whirling snow can make you blind; the wind will freeze the blood in your veins, and you can't find your way anywhere! Expedition leaders check and follow the daily weather forecasts that are available at Base Camp, but one must always keep an eye on the mountain too. Expeditions sometimes share weather reports or download them on satellite phones. One must look for long, extended changes in the weather pattern: four or five continuous days of high or low figures is often a good chance of good or bad weather. They use this information to rest, descend or to climb. Conditions become even more difficult in the 'death zone' (above 8,000 metre) and the bodies of those who perish remain there. Survivors find it difficult and very exhausting to bring them down. Some corpses are visible from standard climbing routes.

You feel small looking at that immense mountain tower over you, and think of all the stories and the legends that are associated with it.

18 May to 22 May 2010

Summit Push

On 18 May, having done our rotations, practice climbs to Island Peak and Kala Patthar, we set off for Camp II. The moment we had been waiting for had finally come—we were going to make our bid for the summit over the next four days. We were now closer than we had ever been in setting foot on the summit.

We made for the summit only after all of us were properly acclimatized to the altitude, something that took us well over a month. The final push is the toughest and the most challenging part of the entire expedition. It tests all your skills and you will find yourself praying for all the luck you can get. You go from Base Camp up to the last camp (in about three days), then you leave your tent at midnight, try to get to the summit and return to the tents before nightfall.

If it sounds simple, it isn't!

18 MAY

I hadn't been able to sleep the night before. I was excited as well as nervous. The goal, which we had all been waiting to fulfil, was now within reach. We would head for the Icefall and this time it would be totally different. It would be the last time I'd be going up the Icefall if all went well. There were too many thoughts in my mind. When Tarche, the cook boy, came to my tent to tell me it was time, I took all my gear and went into the dining tent to find Dawa already there by the heater. He looked at me and smiled. Soon we were joined by the whole team. Everybody appeared raring to go. As was our practice, before leaving for Camp I we went to the stupa and bowed in respect. I remembered every prayer I had learnt because I so wanted this climb to be the best one I had ever attempted.

We set off from Base Camp and reached Camp I by 8.45 a.m. I was the first one to reach Camp I. We rested there for a while. I didn't want to hurry, remembering the last time we had done so, and I had begun to feel unwell soon after. We took our time, ate the apples our cook had given us. And because I was still hungry, I took a packet of dry Maggi noodles, crushed it and mixed the packet of masala powder in it. It tasted so good! Dry instant noodles, you should all try it some time! Soon Mika and Timmo also arrived. Daju and I set off for Camp II. The walk that had been so difficult earlier seemed interesting today. I wasn't tired but was feeling good walking through the vast snow patch and sweating profusely.

The walk from Camp I to Camp II takes climbers through the glacial valley of Western Cwm. From here, climbers have a stupendous view of the upper 8,000 feet of Everest—the first sight of the Everest's upper slopes since arriving at Base Camp. The last 5,000 feet on Everest, including its summit that looks like a black pyramid summit, are not visible from Base Camp. Some of the most difficult days on Everest are in the Western Cwm, when on a windless day it is desperately hot. The valley's structure means there is little wind and the intense sunlight at such a high altitude can make it uncomfortably hot.

We reached Camp II at 2.40 p.m. and had some juice. Daju asked if I had a headache and I said no. He laughed and said that was just as he had expected! After depositing all my gear in my tent, restless as always I rushed outside to see if the others had reached or anyone from the other expeditions was around. But there was no one I knew, so I went to the kitchen tent and looked around, and to my surprise I saw a carton full of Maggi noodles again! Nothing could have made me happier! All this while, they had been my sole source of energy and I was so thrilled to see so many packets of them here.

19 MAY

We rested for most of the day. I was looking forward to the next day when we would begin ascending again, but I was apprehensive too. This time we would head for Camp III, scaling first the dreaded Lhotse wall that had posed such problems for us on the last occasion. With this mixture of apprehension and hope in my mind, I went to sleep for the night.

The western flank of Lhotse is called the Lhotse Face and is an unavoidable part of the traditional south-east route up Everest. From its base to the top, the Lhotse Face rises some 3,700 feet. The entire route is fixed with ropes, and climbers must follow a rhythm of pulling and stepping up, then lodging one's front points into the hard blue ice. Camp III sits at 7,470 metre (24,500 feet) about halfway up the Lhotse Face.

20 MAY

The cook came to wake me up. I had overslept a bit for all the other climbers were awake and ready to set out. I rushed to the dining tent where everyone was already eating their food silently. It seemed to me they were all saving their energy for the big ice wall that promised to be the biggest obstacle in today's climb—the Lhoste wall!

The climb towards the wall was a long and gradual one. I was indeed a bit tired, but the growing excitement as the wall neared took it all away. At the base of the Lhotse wall there was a big crevasse.

We started ascending the Lhotse wall. It was very tiring but we had to keep moving. The whole weight of your body rests on your arms. The Lhotse wall is an eighty-degree straight wall and climbing it saw the most exciting and tiring moments of my life. By the time we reached the halfway mark, I was so tired I was unable to take another step; it seemed next to impossible. The vast big wall was never-ending. There were moments when I just wanted to go back home and fall asleep on my bed. I felt like running away from the mountains forever.

But then it had been the same hunger, the thirst for adventure, that had drawn me to the mountains in the first place. So I began to pep myself up by talking to myself like a madman! I had to do this for there was really no one else who could urge me on. Daju was with me but he was very quiet too. I talked to myself, 'Come on Arjun, you can do it! This is your dream. . . and now you are living your dream. Such small things should not stop you, come on!'

And so shouting my way through I started walking again. I took deep breaths with every step. I was wishing God had been kinder and given me bigger nostrils! At least this would have helped me breathe better at high altitudes. In this manner, slowly and steadily, I reached Camp III.

Camp III is always one of the most difficult camps to set up. It is on a very steep slope. We had to hold on to the rope and stand outside our tents to fix these. It took us two hours to set up one tent. Daju and I were very tired by the end. In our tent, Daju asked me to remove my oxygen mask, then he brought an oxygen bottle and fixed it to my cylinder. We were at an altitude of 7,300 metre and I was feeling perfectly fine. But Daju assured me I would feel much stronger with the supplementary oxygen. We boiled water and took out our dry rations. These were given to every climber. One pack had two meals, some toffees, sweets and an energy drink. It was more than enough for two people. But I was so hungry that I even ate Daju's share because he wasn't much hungry.

It was very windy outside in Camp III. The whole tent shook as if were travelling in one of our passenger trains. It got very cold at night. Having the oxygen mask on was tiresome and sleeping with the oxygen pipes running between your lips to the cylinder was irritating. I had rested a lot but still was unable to sleep well that night on Camp III.

The Mysterious Footsteps

We had gone to sleep early; everyone up in the mountain does. It was a cold night and we were in our tents; no one even dared go outside. Not just because of the snow, but at these altitudes, in that atmosphere of thinning oxygen, even the shortest stroll outside can be exhausting. Altitude can do strange things with the body and the mind. It can also cause hallucinations, and people have problems sleeping.

The Sherpas in their tent next to mine had also curled up and fallen asleep, when we all heard the footsteps. Not slow, soft ones, for footsteps on the hard snow never sound like that. This was a slow, deliberate tramping. Whoever it was outside must be pretty crazy, we thought. Except that we knew it couldn't be one of us or anyone from the other expeditions. There were experienced climbers amongst us, who knew better than to venture out at such a time, in such weather.

We thought no more of it that night and the next day resumed our climb up the Everest. Whoever it was who had come by the night before had now disappeared. The slopes of the Everest abound in dead climbers, who remain lost and buried in the snow for years, even decades. Sometimes they reappear, their limbs sticking out of crevasses that have suddenly opened up. And the Sherpas believe their spirits roam around the mountain that claimed their lives.

21 MAY

We got up early and it was terribly cold. My hands looked set to freeze, and they were paining from the cold as well. Daju helped me by rubbing my hands. When my hands were warm enough I helped rub his hands in turn. We had to always keep our toes and fingers moving so that the blood circulation was not interrupted. It was a big job going out in the morning to relieve ourselves. We used the rest top bags that had been given us. But we were also wearing our down suits. It was terribly difficult doing routine body functions with that entire suit on. Besides, it was a steep slope so things were doubly difficult. When we were ready finally, we began our climb for the day. We were headed for South Col or Camp IV. It was only seven in the morning and it would soon get tougher and tougher. I was walking with an oxygen bottle in my bag. I found it very irritating to walk with the mask on, but I had no choice. It would help me acclimatize to the high altitude.

At 10.18 on the dot, we reach the Yellow Band area. This is halfway up the route to Camp IV. The Yellow Band is very distinctive; it is a sedimentary sandstone rock on the Lhotse Face that needs about 100 metre of rope to traverse it. This is the first rock a climber crosses as he makes his way up the Everest. Some of the team members who had permits for Lhotse left us here.

Climbing the Yellow Band took more than normal climbing skills because it is a huge rock structure. With all one's gear on and those big boots with crampons, it is indeed a strenuous task to climb it at such heights. It's difficult to get a grip on the hard rock with spikes on; you keep slipping all the time, and hold on to the ropes for dear life while trying to keep scary thoughts away from your mind. Climbers must also use ropes to get across the Geneva Spur to reach Camp IV. All this really drains the energy but I thought only of the goal ahead.

The sight of another dead climber, his body hanging from the Lhotse Face, really threw me off kilter. I felt really bad. I could not do anything for the climber, only paused briefly and prayed for his soul. It must have been unthinkably sad for his family who could not even see him one last time, and there he was, clinging to the rock face while every climber only gave him a passing glance.

A little less than two hours later we reached the Geneva Spur. It was almost noon. The Geneva Spur was named thus by a Swiss expedition in 1952, and is a hammer-shaped black rock that climbers scramble up with fixed ropes. Its face is steep and snow-covered. The spur begins at about 24,000 feet and is the last major hurdle before reaching Camp IV, only twenty minutes or so later, the last camp on Everest.

Once we reached, Daju made radio contact with Camp II. His voice was quite weak and breathless as he said, 'We have reached the top of Geneva Spur.' Those hearing him back in camp were delighted. We were the first of all team members to reach this place, perhaps one of the first people from all teams to do so that day.

Distress Call

Once on the Spur, we had now entered the 'death zone'. We were at 8,016 metre and I was feeling very weak. I found my pace had slowed considerably, and my toes too were getting cold. I could feel my hands losing their grip on the rope but I could not really understand what was actually happening. I would often take a break, or pause for breath after every few steps. Soon, after every step I had to stop to catch my breath! I realized soon enough something was wrong.

My glasses had glazed over, and I suddenly found myself keeling over. I tried to call out but even my voice seemed strangled, the effort to speak made me double over again. Daju was behind me, but my shouts couldn't even reach him. I looked down towards Daju but he also seemed very tired. He was looking down and climbing! But soon he caught up and saw I had fallen on my knees. He gestured to me asking what was wrong, but of course being an experienced man of the mountains, he guessed what it was as well. I remember vaguely that I replied, 'I can't breathe, I am going to die!'

I was now breathing like an asthma patient. Daju looked me over carefully and then asked me to wait. He checked my cylinder and then my equipment and pointed out that the valve leading to my oxygen mask tube had choked up or frozen in the snow, which had drastically reduced my oxygen supply. This had happened because of the very fast and cold winds on the wall face. He poured hot water from his flask and all of a sudden I was fine and very relieved. He pulled the mask off my face, cleared the snow by blowing deep and hard into it. He gave me some water and we rested for some time. I started to feel normal soon!

I blamed my overconfidence for this having happened, and the incident brought me down to earth, forced me to concentrate. We made it to Camp IV with some arduous climbing but no further mishap.

May 21

Camp IV

We reached South Col or Camp IV at 12.20 p.m., the rest of the team soon after, within an hour or so.

South Col ('Col' is a word for saddle, or pass) is located at 8,000 metre (26,300 feet). Sometimes climbers choose to spend the night here, in the death zone. There is nothing magical about this altitude, for it is from this point onwards that most human bodies lose all ability to acclimatize. The body begins to deteriorate and die—thus the name 'death zone'. The longer a climber stays at this altitude, the more likely illness (high altitude cerebral edema or HACE and high altitude pulmonary oedema or HAPE) or death will occur. Most climbers will use oxygen to climb and sleep at this altitude and above.

Camp IV, located on a plateau, resembles a moonscape. You are at the edge of the atmosphere and the sky here has a strange, dark blue colour. Climbers make their final preparations for the summit here. There is fear and expectation on everyone's face. People don't talk much. Resting in your tent, feeling weak, you try to get some sleep for in a couple of hours you will start to put on your gear for the final part of the adventure—the summit push. Camp IV is also a haven for worn-out climbers on their exhausting descent from summit attempts (both successful and not).

It was also one of the most beautiful places I've ever been to. We were above the level of the clouds, and I could see the clouds stretching out far below, at our feet. It was like a swimming pool of clouds, or like heaven, the way heaven is shown in the films! At this altitude we are much above all the 7,000 metre mountains in the world and only fourteen other peaks from here would be at eye level. It felt great to have reached this far.

At the same time, it was very dispiriting. I realized why people call South Col the world's highest junkyard. It was full of garbage, left behind by old expedition teams and climbers—tents, oxygen bottles and so many more things. Climbers like us were responsible for this state of affairs. It is difficult to bring down garbage from this altitude, as one can barely walk at this altitude. Imagine the effort required to bring back the load of garbage that has accumulated. Humans are not supposed to exist at such high levels anyway, and just to sustain ourselves in such conditions, we are damaging nature as well.

It was so windy it was like being inside a spin drier. It was even more exhausting setting up a tent here. But soon the rest of the team had reached South Col. Apa Sherpa was really pleased to see the good condition I was in considering the harsh conditions at these heights. I took some photos with Timmo and Mika. It was fun but Apa Sherpa reprimanded us in no time. He had considerably more experience as a climber and told us we were tiring ourselves out too soon; we needed to conserve all our energy for the summit climb.

I soon realized the truth of what he said. Small things like drinking water, even opening the tent zipper to get in or out, getting up after resting—every small activity took lots of time. We had to pause every few seconds to catch our breath.

And besides all this, I was very hungry! Daju and everyone else were amazed at my appetite. At the death zone, most people lose their appetite. But amazingly, I felt fine. The food I took in would have served four people at these heights. Even Sherpas find it difficult to sleep here, but I was soon snoring away. Daju didn't know whether to be amused or to envy my ability.

I was sharing my tent with David Leano and Apa. We were resting when all of a sudden David piped up, 'Hey Arjun, do you want to speak to your parents at home?' Of course I jumped at that, said yes but begged him not to tease me. 'I know I can't speak to them here.' But David only grinned and pulled out his personal satellite phone from his bag.

'Here you go!' he said, extending it towards me. I snatched the phone from his hand before he could change his mind. I dialled home too excited for words. I knew my parents, especially my Mom, would be very worried. And then I thought I did a wrong thing by calling her because she got even more worried after my call. The first thing I told her when I heard her voice was, 'Mom, this is the highest phone call you will ever receive in your life.' She was startled, and at once she was bursting with lots of questions and advice, 'Arjun, where are you? How did you manage to call us? How are you calling? Is everything okay?' I had to do my best to reassure her. I told her we were resting at

Camp IV and would begin walking towards the summit later that night. I also promised her that if I reached the summit with David, I would call her again. She wished me luck but I could hear the fear in her voice. I told her that I was feeling so very good that I could even run up to the summit—which alarmed her even more!

It was really good to speak to her and get news from home. I felt re-energized and couldn't thank David enough for making it possible.

Now it was time to rest, but I was too excited thinking of what lay ahead. There were various thoughts in my mind—would I make it to the summit, would I even survive, would I come back safe with all my fingers and toes intact and not lost to frostbite? I fell asleep with such scary thoughts. Next thing I remember was Apa waking me, with the words, 'Come on Arjun, it's time.'

Leaving Camp IV

The time was around 8 p.m., on 21 May. I woke up and looked outside. Even unzipping the tent left me exhausted. I understood now why we had been woken so early. All the climbing gear that usually takes around ten minutes to put on would take almost an hour and leave one exhausted with the effort. Small things such as wearing shoes, getting up, putting on your harness made me feel as if I had just run the marathon! Then, as I bent to wear my boots with my brand new summit socks that consisted of two layers, I found to my dismay that my leg just wasn't fitting into the boots with those thick socks. I was really worried. I tried again but nothing worked. I realized I should have taken socks of a different size and that I was in for trouble now.

Apa saw my expression and knew something was wrong. As with most things, Apa had a solution for this problem as well. He inquired if I had a pair of new normal thick cotton socks and if so, I was to wear them, but I had to return as soon as I felt my toes getting really cold. Apa said something I will always remember, 'The mountains are always there, but we have only one life!' I agreed totally!

Apa Sherpa was right as usual. It always helps to be sensible while climbing. You must also take control of your own gear and climbing decisions. To turn around means you still have other attempts later. It's far wiser to fail than to die. In truth, many good Everest climbers have turned around before reaching the summit. For example, the great Italian climber Reinhold Messner's summit ratio in the Himalayas is 1:3.

With great effort I got ready and just when we were finally about to make a move, it began snowing. We were very disappointed. We had so believed the weather report that had indicated a clear night ahead that this wasn't what we had expected. Only Apa stayed calm as ever. He went out and took a look around. When he came back, all he said was, 'Don't worry. It will stop snowing in an hour.' We had no choice but to repose total faith in him. After having summited Everest nineteen times, Apa Sherpa was the most experienced person on the whole mountain with us. We would trust him with our lives.

Finally, the hour came. At about 10 p.m. we stepped out in the night. It was still snowing, but lightly, as we started to walk towards our final destination. And as soon as we started to climb, it stopped snowing! I was amazed to see how much Apa's experience had helped us.

I had been told over and over again that there are some things to remember before setting out. Go over your gear while there's still light. Have everything neatly organized. Drink lots of fluid, especially hot fluids, on the climb. Get your axe ready. The cold, scary darkness outside is anything but inviting, but as soon as you start out on the climb you will feel much better. Fear is always worse than reality.

Climbing up the dark mountain in the solitary pool of light from the head torch made me yearn for the dawn. When it would come, a few hours later, it would perhaps be the best dawn that I'll ever see. The wall towards the summit is steep and dark. In the death zone, I couldn't help thinking that within the next forty-eight hours there was a very real risk that I might not live.

Leaving Camp IV, there's a little bit of a down slope, with the uphill side to the left. There's usually snow on the ledges to walk down on, interspersed with rock, along with some fixed rope. Fortunately it's not too steep, but there is a lot of exposed rock and people are usually tired when walking down from camp. A small climb above camp, you look down to the Tibetan plateau with its vast brown plains, white glaciers and the other alpine giants—Kanchenjunga, Lhotse, Makalu—in the distance. It's all magical and unreal.

When to Climb

What climbers primarily look for is a prolonged period (four to five days) of stable weather with no jet stream winds. This is called 'the window'. Jet stream winds are winds that blow at great speed in the higher reaches of the atmosphere; their movement directly influences weather patterns across the world. Usually this 'window' comes every year at about the same time, around the third or fourth week of May, and lasts for about a week. To find a window, it is important to study the movement of the monsoons. When it moves north from the Bay of Bengal, this powerful weather system will push the jet wind to the north, thereby weakening its effect a bit in the Himalayas. This helps create a period of perfect weather. Sometimes there is a period of weak winds and good weather in the beginning of May. Climbers should be ready for a summit attempt from the 1st of May to take advantage of this.

If they don't summit on this first, early attempt, there will be plenty of time to go down the valley for a week's rest, and then to head back up for a new attempt at the end of the month.

The wind force forecast should definitely not exceed 40 mph when going for the summit. Mountaineers can maybe make it in 50, but then you are extremely exposed to wind-chill and exhaustion.

On the Way to the Summit

In the distance not too far away, we could see a ladder of light also moving upwards. It was the flickering light from the head torches of other climbers. Otherwise it was completely silent. Nobody was talking. We kept climbing, awaiting the first ray of dawn. It was desperately cold, and the ground at parts very icy. The ice axe and the crampons cut deep into the ice.

A cold, white moon rose from below, but we hardly glanced at it or even at the bright twinkle of the universe above. The adrenaline keeps your body moving. Apa's knowledge and experience again helped our team avoid the traffic jam and the big line of climbers as we made our way up. We were ahead of every other team that night. Daju and me were among the first fifteen climbers. After some time I looked back and saw the big trail of head lamps behind us.

I never thought I could go so slow. I stopped to rest after every two steps. I had to pace my body so that I didn't tire easily and at the same time not let my body cool down. The winds were also terrible! It seemed someone was pulling me from behind all the time and left me aching all over.

We kicked our feet and wriggled our toes repeatedly to beat the frostbite. Soon we were at the Balcony, at 8,443 metre (27,700 feet), to have a short rest and change to a new oxygen bottle. This is the only place where you can actually sit and rest comfortably. Daju and I drank some hot water, rested a bit before we resumed the climb again. It was a very steep climb from now on. At many places we had to move over small rock patches, which was tiring at this altitude. I don't know how my body responded or moved. I saw the big line of climbers following us and didn't want to get stuck in the traffic with so many climbers on the same line. Then I realized I was becoming weaker and weaker with every step I took. The same thing had happened as before—my mask had frozen up again! At least I had learnt from seeing Daju clear my mask the last time, and despite my growing exhaustion I took out my mask and blew through it, and then moved on.

In these difficult conditions, you have to start playing games with your mind. The Everest not only tests your physical fitness but also how tough you are mentally. After walking for more than five hours, the pain and the exhaustion can be unbearable. Taking the next step seems nearly impossible. So you carry on by giving your mind short-term goals; such as will I be able to take the next three steps? Or, okay here we go, 1 . . . 2 . . . 3 steps more, yes I did it. You egg yourself on constantly. Every word I spoke to myself fuelled me to take one more step, and in this way, I advanced one step at a time.

From the Balcony, the snow ridge rises 1,000 feet to the South Summit and arcs to the north. At around 5.40 a.m. we reached the South Summit. On reaching there I bent down to take a deep breath. When I looked up again, the whole universe stretched out before me! I could see the Milky Way scattered all over the sky. We were at such a great height that all the clouds were below me, and I could see stars of every colour. I saw a shooting star also, and then I realized that it was a rain of shooting stars. I saw so many of them in a short period of time that I ran out of wishes too soon!

The South Summit is a small table-size dome of snow and ice at 8,748 metre (28,700 feet). From here the climbers can see the final obstacles ahead of them: the Cornice Traverse or the Knife Ridge, the Hillary Step, and the final slopes to the summit, now less than 100 metre away. I began to enjoy the view, and the possibility of success. Several hundred feet below the South Summit, there is a series of rock steps that often forces climbers to the east and into waist-deep snow. This can often be the most strenuous and dangerous section of the climb, because the wind-deposited snow can be avalanche prone.

But the view had once again re-energized me. On seeing the summit not far away, I started climbing towards it. I still remember those next few minutes. It was like I was nearly there but still not reaching it!

From the South Summit we climbed to the Cornice Traverse or the Knife Ridge, a horizontal face of snow and rock. I gasped on seeing it. It is steep and looks truly nasty. The ridge towers almost freely over Nepal and Tibet—it's sharp and very steep. Hillary Step is in the middle somewhere, a rock climb in the sky.

I stepped on to the ridge via a small, half-open tunnel from South Summit. I had to climb with my crampons at a sharp angle. If there is a lot of snow, the ridge could be almost wide and quite nice. Occasionally, the snow can give way and you slip for a scary second. This is not a place to climb without fixing ropes. Climbers must clip in carefully, focus on each step and keep moving, till they make it finally to the Hillary Step.

The Hillary Step is at an altitude of 8,790 metre (28,840 feet) and stretches over 40 feet. It is very difficult to cross. Now because of global warming and other environmental issues the entire Hillary Step, which once used to be covered with snow, is totally exposed. All the snow on it has melted, making it harder for climbers to traverse it. My instructors at NIM had warned me of this moment. They had told me that the Hillary Step asked a lot of any climber, but that it was important to make it through the Step. Reaching the Hillary Step means you are very close to your destination. Make your mind strong and keep walking! I remembered this piece of advice and it helped me get over the Hillary Step.

The Step is climbed with fixed ropes, so that only one climber can ascend or descend at a time. It is named after Sir Edmund Hillary. Though the Hillary Step would not be difficult at sea level for experienced climbers, at Everest's altitude, it is considered the most technically challenging aspect of the climb. While today's climbers use a fixed rope up here to ascend the Step, Hillary and Tenzing had climbed this impressive obstacle without fixed ropes and using ice climbing equipment that is primitive by today's standards.

From the Hillary Step, climbers must trek the final feet to reach the summit. I could see the summit now just in front of me. I just had to go down a bit and then a small climb to reach the real summit! Every step I took towards it brought fresh tears to my eyes. The dream I had been living with for the past six years was finally going to come true in a few moments. I didn't know what I would do once I reached the summit, but I was so happy!

After the Hillary Step, one sees white, strange wave-formations of frozen snow pointing out from the summit. We kept climbing towards them. This section is not usually roped, but it isn't too steep. Near the top are survey and scientific equipment, prayer flags, discarded oxygen bottles, and a few other small items and mementoes left by climbers. Then we reach another white edge, but this time it doesn't stretch too far; instead it slopes downwards. We were peeking down at the north side of Everest, and so we had finally reached!

22 MAY

On Top of the World

I finally reached the summit at 6.18 a.m. on 22 May, a day I shall never forget. My dream had come true. I was crying like a baby and also laughing. Daju was just behind me and as soon as he saw me on the summit he lowered his mask and cheered for me, still about 20 feet away from the summit. The shout must have resounded in the distance. Then he too joined me there.

I still remember every second I spent there. I was finally on the top of the world! There was a Buddha statue there and I headed straight towards it and bowed low. As I raised my head, I saw the most wondrous sight ever: the sunrise! Even the sun was below me, and as it slowly rose, every mountain peak covered by the darkness slowly began glowing like gold. Nothing obstructed my view across miles and miles. I could see the curvature of the earth's surface.

We briefly enjoyed the view from 8,848 metre (29,028 feet), as we knew we couldn't stay too long. From here, we could see across the Tibetan Plateau, towards the other Himalayan peaks of Cho Oyu, Makalu and Kanchenjunga. It's a wonderful 360 degree view.

I remembered everyone, every person who had helped me achieve this dream. It was so cold I couldn't even get goose pimples; besides my skin was also stiff. I was hoping there was some way I could call up home. I was among the first fifteen climbers to summit that day, the only Indian among them. I felt proud as I placed the Indian flag on the summit. I had my oxygen mask on so I started to sing the national anthem in my mind! Daju too sang some Tibetan prayers, where he thanked the mountain goddess for a safe climb. I quickly emptied my water bottle and filled it with the snow on the summit and picked up a small piece of rock as a memory to last me a lifetime! But when the time came to take pictures, another tragedy happened. I switched on my camera and all I read was the message, 'battery exhausted'. It was too ironic a situation.

Because of the low temperature and the pressure, the battery had frozen. I quickly took off my gloves and took out the battery from my camera and rubbed it for a few moments with my hands. Fortunately, it worked for a few seconds and I was lucky enough to get some summit pictures.

Coming Down

The night is always the best time to attempt an Everest push. If you stand on the summit later in the day your brain will be addled from the lack of oxygen and you will be in danger of not getting back to camp before nightfall. The risk of staying at the summit and the exhaustion from achieving the summit is too great. As the list of deaths attests, getting down safely can be as dangerous as getting up. Most accidents occur while climbing down. I had to make sure I had enough oxygen and not relax for one moment. I was not feeling good about going back but there was the fear in my mind that it is always more difficult to descend than to climb up. Plus I was in the death zone; the lesser time we spent there, the better it was for all of us. At the same time I felt light, airy and on top of the world still in many ways.

As soon as we reached the Hillary Step on our way back, I saw the long line of people coming up! It was terrifying to see so many climbers cramped in such a narrow space. It was very difficult climbing past them, and overtaking was impossible. I got a bit delayed but managed to avoid getting caught in that human traffic jam. The South Summit was full of tired people resting, some of them not in a very good condition. I could see the ones who would definitely not make it to the summit. It was disheartening to see them just standing at one place totally exhausted, not able to take even a step further.

I realized as I descended the truth of why coming down is that much more difficult. My legs and hands began to pain. Basically I was finished for the day. I reached Camp IV before noon, and Daju and I stopped for water and had some biscuits.

I didn't want to spend much time in the death zone and so decided to go down to Camp II that very day. Usually climbers come down to Camp IV, spend a night there and return to Camp II the next day. But I wasn't really happy with the idea of spending another night in the death zone.

I started walking again. It was getting tougher with every step I took. Around 2 p.m. I was at Camp III and really exhausted. I had been walking since 10 o'clock last night. My legs were hurting badly now. With every step I took on the hard ice, it was as if someone was hammering me on the knees. I found myself wishing for

someone to chop away my legs. I met Tomy and
Yonni at Camp III. Their ascent towards Lhotse
had not been successful. They had fallen short
of ropes at the end, barely a few metres away
from the summit. In spite of this, they were
happy they had made the effort.

Daju was also very tired. He wasn't complaining
about my resting after every few steps but I
could see what he was going through because
of my slow speed. So I told him to go ahead. 'I
know the way, we are anyway close to Camp II,'
I tried to sound reassuring. 'I will come on my
own. You keep walking at your own pace.' He
said, 'No! I am not going to leave you up on this
mountain alone.' So we argued and finally he
gave up. He just looked at me once and started
walking towards Camp II. After some time I
resumed walking at my own slow pace.

After descending a bit from Camp III I was
at the Lhotse wall. I grabbed the rope that I
thought was the correct one and started climbing
down very slowly and carefully. I was tired. My
entire body weight rested on my hands.

But as luck would have it, and as I realized
only when I was halfway across the wall, I had
made the classic climber's mistake. A maze of
fixed ropes had stretched out before me and I
had picked the wrong one. There I was now,
unsure of the way down, and looking down at
the deepest crevasse I had ever seen. The rope
seemed old, and no one was around.

I tried hard not to panic. I knew I had to go back all the way up and come down using the correct rope but I was unable to move myself. I just could not push myself up, not even by a few metres. I had been walking for almost seventeen hours now. I think I was a bit hypoxic also, suffering from a lack of oxygen so my mind wasn't functioning that well. I had very little control over my body.

Below me, I could see the big black hole that stretched away at the very bottom. I had a vision where I saw myself dying for sure that day. There was no one on the whole mountain coming down at this time. It was perhaps 3.30 p.m. Generally everyone stops climbing by 12 or 1 p.m. I knew nobody was going to come and save me that day. I had made a big foolish decision by sending Daju up ahead.

I was slowly losing my grip on the rope. Many strange thoughts started filling my mind. I was thinking of what would happen at home when my folks there got to know about this. Then I had tears in my eyes. I remembered Mom scolding me for many things and how Dad would come to my rescue on these occasions. I thought of my sister who shares all my secrets. I was going to lose all of them in a few more moments. I wasn't scared of dying, but I was feeling bad I could not keep the promise I had made to my mother—of coming back home.

I remembered my Mom giving me her prayer book, the *Hanuman Chalisa*. I had had an argument with her about it, because I didn't want to take it along. 'What would I do with it on the mountain?' I asked, but she had insisted and made me keep it in my bag.

I just touched my bag now and prayed to God. I wanted to be saved and I prayed hard. I don't know how long I stood there, at times wondering if I should just leave the rope and let go. I hung there, wondering about the mountains, my family and my friends. I thought of the songs I wanted to sing and never had. I had always wanted to perform in front of a big audience and now the earth and the mountains stretched away from me in a vast icy emptiness. But at least the mountains could listen to me, I thought. The song that came to mind was 'Summer of 69', my favourite Bryan Adams number.

So I started to sing, and then was interrupted by a voice from behind!

'Hey, what are you doing here? And at this time alone! Where is your Sherpa?'

Believe me, I have never felt so happy in my whole life to hear and then see a Sherpa approach. He was totally snow burnt. He was the saviour God had sent for me. I realized he was Cleo's Sherpa from our team who had taken a different route to climb Lhotse. She had had two Sherpas with her. I was so happy to see Sherpa Lakhpa, which was his name, that I couldn't stop singing! I guess Lakhpa thought I had totally lost it but he saw the predicament I was in and came to my rescue.

I had somehow forgotten I had a jumar that could have made my going back up a little bit easier. In my hypoxic state, I just could not think clearly.

I locked my jumar on to the rope and with Lakhpa's help I was back and holding on to the right rope this time. The two of us didn't speak much as we headed straight down the wall. Finally, after climbing for nearly nineteen and a half hours I reached Camp II. I could not thank Lakhpa enough. This is one Sherpa, besides Daju, who I cannot forget in my entire life.

THE DREAM OF THE EVEREST

Climbing the Everest is not merely about a dream, but also acting on it. Everest is our highest mountain and the climb has an everlasting, profound impact on most Everest climbers' lives. The Everest is a graceful, gentle mountain, even though it occasionally keeps some of us forever when some climbers fail to make it back. In return, Everest offers the lucky rest a tremendous insight into ourselves as we climbers are tried in very harsh situations. Everest also reveals the true soul of nature, in all its beauty, temper and might. Finally, Everest shows you the grace of great dreams, fears that are overcome and, sometimes, triumph following the most desperate of outlooks.

Reaching the summit of Everest is not merely an achievement, but an experience to be savoured, to be relived, cherished, and it has become an inspiration for all that I will do next. As valuable and worth treasuring are the moments on the way; the time I spent with my fellow climbers, the camaraderie we shared, the stories we exchanged, the fear, the laughter, the jokes, and the joy of shared achievement.

I also realized I need to give back to the mountain in some way. Dawa Steven saw the impact global warming and climate change have had on the Everest, which is why he launched the Eco Everest Expedition in 2008. I am happy to have been a part of it in 2010, and to do my share in cleaning up the Base Camp.

Junko Tabei, who in 1975 became the first woman to climb Everest and after that went on to climb the 'seven summits' across the world, has written extensively on the perils of environmental damage to the Everest. She wrote about the Gasherbrum base camp located at an elevation of 17,060 feet in the Karakoram, where 'the number of crows and butterflies have increased. I have witnessed large numbers of crows attracted by food and observed butterflies flying around. A few porters said they had seen bears and leopards a long time ago. . . The high altitude porters and guides said that as a result of food being left behind here, the number of ibexes had increased. Several times from inside my tent I saw groups of ibexes leisurely walking on rocks far above. I was told, however, that wild yaks and tigers no longer exist here. . .' Mount Everest is one of Earth's greatest treasures, considered sacred by untold numbers of people. The protection of its natural environment is the duty of visiting mountaineers.

The mountains may look remote and unshakeable but I returned aware of their fragility. We live in a symbiotic relationship with nature, and the more we take care of it and respect it, the more secure our lives are and those of future generations. The effects of global warming can still be stemmed. We need to be responsible, caring and concerned citizens of the Earth. Looking down from the Everest summit, I felt as though the earth belonged to me, and I belonged to it, and was part of it. It's an overwhelming feeling.

FUTURE PLANS

Being on Everest is the experience of a lifetime and yet it has fuelled my ambitions like nothing else. Once on top of the world, you think of all the other mountain peaks to be climbed, all the other adventures yet to be experienced!

Mountaineering isn't just a sport, it becomes for many a lifelong passion and a commitment. For those not content simply to climb Mount Everest, there are other challenges available. Everest is one of the Seven Summits, the highest point on each of the seven continents. More than 164 people are on the Seven Summiteers list.

If super-high altitude is your thing, you can join the elite group of twelve people who have climbed all fourteen of the world's peaks over 8,000 metre. I hope I can do this one day. My immediate goal, besides more practical things like preparing for my class XII board exams, is to try and aim for the mini Grand Slam that includes the conquest of the two Poles, besides the Everest.

Notes on Mount Everest

How Mount Everest was Formed

Shaped roughly like a pyramid, and covered by glaciers, Mount Everest is part of the Himalayan mountain range that stands on and forms the border between Nepal and Tibet. The Himalayas are 'fold mountains' that were formed ('folded up') millions of years ago by the slow process of continental drift. This happened over several millions of years. At one time, the Tethys Sea separated the region of South Asia from the Asian continent. Over time, with the drift, the Indian subcontinent moved towards the Asian mainland and the sea was pushed upwards to form a series of parallel ridges, or folds. Marine fossils can still be found on the Himalayas.

The Himalayas are a young mountain chain, having formed only 60 million years ago. In fact, the Himalayas are still growing and because they have been geologically proven to be still growing, the height of Everest has been disputed. When originally surveyed, Mount Everest was estimated at 8,848 metre. It is believed to have grown by as much as 2 metre since then. On 11 November 1999, the National Geographic Society and Bradford Washburn, an American explorer and mountaineer who died in 2007, announced the new height of Everest as 8,850 metre, based on GPS readings. On 5 May 1999, American and Nepalese climbers had successfully placed GPS equipment on the Everest peak. Though there has been disagreement on the Everest's height between Nepal and China, this dispute has only recently been settled. So most recent maps of China and Nepal show 8,848 metre as the height of the Everest. This figure is the one to go with until a new complete survey of the area is done.

How the Everest Got Its Name

In 1856, the Great Trigonometric Survey of India established the first published height of Everest, then known as Peak XV, at 8,840 metre (29,002 feet). In 1865, Everest was given its official English name by the Royal Geographical Society in London on the recommendation of Andrew

Waugh, the British Surveyor General of India at the time. George Everest had been Waugh's predecessor as Surveyor General of India.

The name Chomolangma had been in common use by Tibetans for centuries. At that time Nepal and Tibet were closed to foreigners. In 1852, four years before it was officially named, Radhanath Sikdar, an Indian mathematician and surveyor stationed at the headquarters of the Great Trignometric Survey of India, was the first to identify Everest as the world's highest peak using trigonometric calculations based on earlier measurements. An official announcement that Peak XV was the highest was delayed for several years as the calculations were verified and then finally announced in March 1856.

WHAT DOES ONE EAT AT HIGH ALTITUDES?

The good news about an Everest diet is that you can follow the opposite of everything your doctor told you. Bring all the fatty stuff you think you like but it's important to eat sensibly too. Eat lots of local vegetables (onions, cabbage, carrots). The expedition cook offers heated canned fruit, which is tasteless but adds bulk to the diet. Garlic is also excellent for altitude adaptation because it thins the blood. Sherpas chew on it constantly and so should you. Processed cheese, salami, peanut butter, jam, tinned ham, tinned meals, snacks, candy and chocolate are all useful items to stock up on.

For camps at high altitudes, instant soups, cheese cubes, chocolate, hot chocolate powder, milk powder, some coffee and tea, cereals and oatmeal for breakfast also help. Instant packed foods such as rice/pasta casseroles or instant soups requiring a few minutes to cook can also be eaten. And of course there's always instant noodles, that came to my rescue on many an occasion! On the climbs, candy bars, nuts, crackers, all help. Sherpas eat boiled eggs on climbing. I had them too, with some salt I had wrapped in a plastic bag along with a piece of cheese and bread.

The more 'real' food you eat at altitude the better you'll perform. Vegetables like carrots, as well as cubed cheese and energy drinks, are useful.

The most important thing is to drink plenty of water. There may be a variety of altitude hazards to your health and many ways to prevent and cure, but a simple way of doing so is by drinking lots of water. High altitude health problems like headache, oedema, frostbite, confusion are actually more often related to dehydration than lack of oxygen. Water helps you cope with symptoms of altitude sickness.

THE PIONEERS

In 1885, in a book called *Above the Snow Line* a writer called Clinton Thomas Dent suggested that climbing Mount Everest was possible. In 1921, the northern approach to the mountain, from the Tibet side, was discovered by George Mallory. This was an exploratory British expedition and Mallory became the first European to set foot on Everest's flanks.

Mallory returned in 1922 as part of a second British expedition. This time they were trying to reach the summit. On 22 May, they climbed to 8,170 metre (26,800 feet) on the North Ridge before retreating. On 7 June, George Mallory led a third attempt but set off an avalanche, killing seven Sherpa climbers. Two years later in 1924, still drawn by the irresistible lure of the Himalayas, Mallory returned again, but this time the consequences would be tragic. On 8 June, Mallory and a team member called Andrew Irvine attempted the summit. They were last seen at 26,000 feet on the ridge near the base of the final pyramid. The mystery about whether they reached the top or made it back after the First Step continues. Mallory's body was discovered finally on 1 May 1999, by an expedition called the Mallory and Irvine Research Expedition led by Eric Simonson.

Mallory's grandson, also called George Mallory, reached the summit of Everest in 1995 via the North Ridge with six other climbers as part of the American Everest Expedition 1995. He left a picture of his grandparents at the summit citing 'unfinished business'.

In 1935, Eric Shipton led a small reconnaissance expedition to examine alternative possible routes on the mountain. Shipton established that an ascent from the Western Cwm would be possible if entry from the Nepalese side could be made. This would be the route by which Everest would finally be climbed in 1953. Shipton's expedition is also notable as the first visit to Everest for Tenzing Norgay, who was engaged as one of the porters. In 1950, Nepal opened its borders to foreigners. That year, another expedition led by Shipton, and including Edmund Hillary, travelled into Nepal to survey a new route via the southern face. On 30 September at 6,100 metre (20,000 feet) on Pumori, Shipton and Hillary saw the entire Western Cwm and concluded that climbing Everest was possible from the Cwm to the west face of Lhotse, followed by moving up to the South Col.

1953 was a watershed year, when Tenzing and Hillary, as part of a British expedition to the Everest led by John Hunt, made it to the top. The summit was finally reached at 11:30 a.m. local time on 29 May 1953 by Edmund Hillary from New Zealand and Tenzing Norgay from Nepal taking the South Col route. They paused at the summit to take photographs and buried a few sweets and a small cross in the snow before coming down.

1963 saw the first ascent by an American, Jim Whittaker, accompanied by Nawang Gombu, a Sherpa who later went on to become the first man to climb Everest twice; he did so again in 1965, when he reached the summit on 20 May. This time he was part of a twenty-one-man Indian expedition, led by Lieutenant Commander M.S. Kohli, that succeeded in putting nine men on the summit. On 16 May 1975, Junko Tabei of Japan became the first woman on the summit. The first ascent without supplemental oxygen was made in 1978, when Reinhold Messner from Italy and Peter Habeler (Austria) reached the summit. In 1984, on 23 May, Bachendri Pal climbing via the standard south-east ridge route became the first Indian woman to reach the Everest.

On 22 May 2010, some time after my summit climb which was a world record, a thirteen-year-old American boy, Jordan Romero, climbed the Everest using the North Ridge route via Tibet. I am now the youngest Indian to have reached the Everest summit, at the age of sixteen years, eleven months and eighteen days!